*The Sexual Education
of Edith Wharton*

Edith Wharton, Christmas 1905. Courtesy, Lilly Library,
Indiana University.

The Sexual Education
of Edith Wharton

Gloria C. Erlich

UNIVERSITY OF CALIFORNIA PRESS
BERKELEY LOS ANGELES OXFORD

University of California Press
Berkeley and Los Angeles, California

University of California Press, Ltd.
Oxford, England

© 1992 by
The Regents of the University of California

"Beatrice Palmato" is reprinted here with the permission of the
Edith Wharton estate.

Library of Congress Cataloging-in-Publication Data

Erlich, Gloria C.
  The sexual education of Edith Wharton / Gloria C.
Erlich. p. cm.
  Includes bibliographical references (p.   ) and index.
  ISBN 0-520-07583-8 (cloth)
  1. Wharton, Edith, 1862–1937—Biography—Psychology. 2.
Wharton, Edith, 1862–1937—Knowledge—Psychology. 3. Wharton,
Edith, 1862–1937—Relations with men. 4. Women authors, American—
Sexual behavior. 5. Femininity (Psychology) in literature. 6.
Women authors, American—Psychology. 7. Psychoanalysis and
literature. 8. Women in literature. 9. Sex in literature. I. Title
PS3545.H16Z646   1992
813'.52—dc20   91-16671
                                                                      CIP

Printed in the United States of America
1   2   3   4   5   6   7   8   9

To Phil
In all ways, the foundation

Contents

Illustrations following page 114

Preface

> At first [Freud] took sexuality to be unproblematic:
> what was surprising was the extent to which sexuality
> spread throughout psychological life.
>   Jonathan Lear, *Love and Its Place in Nature*

Lest anyone be deceived, let me state right off that, with the possible exception of the appended fragment that Wharton intended to suppress, this is not an X-rated book. The "sexual education" of my title refers both to mastery of "the facts of life," which was an uncommonly problematic business for Edith Wharton, and to something much larger and more pervasive—akin to Jonathan Lear's idea that "human sexuality is an incarnation of love, a force for unification present wherever there is life."[1] For Edith Wharton sexual education was a lifelong process of coming to terms with the role of love and sensuality in human experience.

This book traces Edith Wharton's erotic development and her use of writing to explore new possibilities for that development. The process starts with flaws in the mother-daughter relationship that derailed her emotional development and caused a massive sexual repression. From this unfortunate beginning, Edith Wharton moved unprepared into a disastrous and celibate marriage, so that her awakening to full sexuality was delayed until her mid-forties.

Childhood deficits left her with special developmental tasks that she performed in her own unusual way. Her inability to acknowledge the most basic facts of human sexuality must have caused great confusion in understanding the world about her—both personal and social relationships—saddling her with many misconceptions that she had to correct. In addition, she had to revise her flawed maternal imagery in order to forge a functional gender identity along with a professional identity. Because sexuality pervades human experience, my story follows several interacting and evolving identity systems—the filial, the sexual, and the creative, each influencing the others.

The book proceeds from the hypothesis that the common social custom by which children receive their primary nurturance from mother surrogates, such as nannies or nursemaids, alters children's maternal imagery and has, therefore, significant influence on their emotional lives. Considering the amount of research currently accorded to mother-infant interactions during the pre-oedipal period, it is surprising how little attention has been given to the consequences of splitting the child's first feelings of attachment among multiple nurturing figures.

The consequences are not uniform or predictable because there are many variables, including social norms, the presence or absence of class difference between the mother and the surrogate (sometimes a family member, often an unmarried aunt), and the child's level of reactivity to this aspect of its environment. In the introduction that follows I adduce testimony about the significance of multiple mothering from a variety of cultures—British, Italian, French, Austrian, and American—admittedly all western and, except for Leonardo da Vinci's Italy, relatively recent, but diverse enough to indicate that whether or not the phenomenon is universal, it is worthy of attention.

The project evolved from my previous book, *Family Themes and Hawthorne's Fiction*.[2] In that book as in this one, I register the impact of a psychic design derived from early family experience on the particular channel and course of an author's creativity. In *Family Themes* I examined the effects of doubled paternal figures on Nathaniel Hawthorne's imagination. His psyche and imagination were affected by the split between his biological father, whom he scarcely knew, and a father-surrogate whom he found oppressive.

In both books I treat doubled parental imagery as a salient

feature in shaping the authors' imaginations without suggesting that split parenting is the sole key to their lives and works. Cultural attitudes toward gender and the profession of authorship play into the entire process. With both Wharton and Hawthorne, the power of social attitudes was reinforced by peculiarities of the family constellation.

Edith Wharton experienced a particularly intense form of the kinds of neurasthenia that Sandra Gilbert and Susan Gubar attribute to nineteenth-century women writers. She suffered for extended periods from eating disorders, hysteria, migraines, claustrophobia, and asthma.[3] Despite her professional success, she never stopped experiencing the "anxiety of authorship" that Gilbert and Gubar find peculiarly intense in women writers. Her individual psychology played into and intensified prevailing social constructions of femininity, creating pressures that she tried to solve by means of her fictive imagination.

Neither biography nor pure literary criticism, this book looks at the continuities between Wharton's life and art. Life and art illuminate each other; neither is privileged over the other, neither subordinate. If *The Sexual Education of Edith Wharton* contributes something to the psychology of love, it does so by reading the letters, memoirs, fiction, and poetry of this very articulate woman as a composite record of her inner and outer life. Indeed, the book studies this writer's use of fiction to rework her maternal imagery, to imagine scripts for future development, and to integrate alienated aspects of her self. This reciprocal method allows us to see not only the autobiographical elements in Edith Wharton's fiction, but the psychic work fiction performed in the construction of the author's selfhood at various stages of the life cycle. To accomplish this, I try to link into one interpretive system several apparently separate domains: family constellation, cognitive style, sexual development, and literary themes.[4]

The first chapter presents Edith Wharton's early family constellation and an overview of its implications for her life and work. It shows that the emotional split between mother and nanny initiated a fairly intransigent psychic split that would later be reflected in Wharton's delayed sexual awakening and celibate marriage. I try to envision how it felt to be this ardent and imaginative girl living within a family and social system that denied both her sexual impulses and her creative urges. These drives merged in her father's library, a "secret garden" where sexual inquiry and ecstatic experiences flowed together. From Wharton's autobiographical statements, her erotic poetry, and the incestuous "Beatrice Palmato" fragment, I identify what appears to be the nucleus of her fantasy life—the displacement of her sexuality onto words and books.

Chapter 2, "On the Threshold," analyzes Wharton's first major novel, *The House of Mirth*, as an extrapolation of the author's family themes and sexual repression. The marriage-seeking heroine is unable to cross the threshold into sexual maturity. Convinced that the novel is driven by the author's own psychological urgencies, I challenge the social-determinist view that it is society that dooms Lily Bart to an untimely death.[5]

At the center of the book stands Chapter 3, "The Passion Experience," which deals with the dynamics of Edith Wharton's belated sexual awakening in a midlife love affair with the bisexual journalist Morton Fullerton, an unlikely pairing that has long puzzled her biographers. This chapter shows how her own imagination had prepared Wharton for her choice of such an amoral libertine and how Fullerton's incestuous inclinations meshed with Wharton's own. She had anticipated such a relationship in "The Touchstone" and would later elaborate on it in *The Reef*.

Chapter 4, "Parental Inscriptions," opens with Wharton's relationships with men after the Fullerton affair and her subsequent divorce, showing how her circle of male friends functioned almost as a composite husband. The works of this major period reflect new reworkings of her familiar motifs—sexual inhibition, incest, and complex variations on split parenthood.

The concluding chapter, "Final Adjustments," shows Edith Wharton using fiction to devise scripts to work through the loneliness and fears of old age. In the Vance Weston novels, *Hudson River Bracketed* and *The Gods Arrive*, Wharton moves from the biological mother to a mythicized and benevolent maternal principle. With this change in maternal imagery she was able to bring her femininity into alignment with her creativity by reinventing herself as a mother whose posterity would consist of books. Over this kunstlerroman of a novelist hovers the generative figure of Emily Lorburn, a woman of letters who presides over her own library and inspires the next generation of writers. In Wharton's posthumous final novel, *The Buccaneers*, her lost nanny returns in the form of a governess, a benign and healing figure who leads a young woman into sexual maturity.

In view of the interlocking of Wharton's affective and professional identities, her greatest creative act may well have been the forging through her own intellect and imagination what life had denied her—an inner mother that would suffice.

Introduction:
On Double Mothering

How was it that hundreds of thousands of mothers,
apparently normal, could simply abandon all loving
and disciplining and company of their little children,
sometimes almost from birth, to the absolute care of
other women, total strangers, nearly always
uneducated?

Jonathan Gathorne-Hardy,
The Rise and Fall of the British Nanny

Interrogation of the commonplace has in recent decades
yielded radical new perspectives for social historians. They
delight in discovering the consequences of practices and beliefs so widely accepted as to be almost invisible at the time—
such as assumptions about gender roles, family structure, and
hygiene, or, more pertinent to the present purpose, the effects
of servants on the life of a family. Biographers and psychoana-
lysts have been slower to recognize that commonplace experiences such as the presence of a servant or a nursemaid in the
household may indeed influence a child's development and
constitute a significant element of a life history.

   In a remarkable piece of social history, *The Rise and Fall of
the British Nanny*, Jonathan Gathorne-Hardy examined the
nanny phenomenon during the late nineteenth and early twentieth centuries in Britain, revealing how multiple mothering
affected the personality, career, and psychosexual lives of
many people, including public figures such as Winston Churchill. The book presents a social history of British upper-class
mores, which fostered the development of a nanny culture. It

also offers a historical and psychological perspective on multiple mothering—ranging from foster care and wet-nursing to communal child-rearing on kibbutzim. Gathorne-Hardy is sensitive to the ways in which the introduction of an alternative nurturing figure affects the dynamics of the family and the future erotic life of the child. He observes that upper-class nanny-reared men tend to feel less sexual potency with their wives than with working-class women, perhaps because the latter remind them of their most intimate early caretakers, their nannies.

Gathorne-Hardy expresses astonishment that Anthony Storr, a psychoanalytic biographer of Winston Churchill, tried to account for Churchill's personality by reference to parental neglect without recognizing the formative role played by his beloved nanny. When queried about this lapse, Storr acknowledged that Nanny Everest had indeed saved young Winston's life but argued that "a Nanny's love never made up for a hostile or neglectful mother because a child always knew the mother was the authority."[1] Storr's claim is true enough, but imperfect compensation for maternal deficiencies does not eliminate the nanny from the psychic picture; it complicates the picture.

A large part of the upper-class English child's socialization was left to its nanny, who tended to be a strict disciplinarian. The classic British nanny, according to Gathorne-Hardy, was probably more repressive than the child's own mother would have been, possibly because of a sexual puritanism among women of the respectable working class. Such women were trained by the nanny culture to perpetuate the values of the ruling class. Nannies and nursemaids were at least as snobbish as their employers and probably more rigid about the social distinctions that discriminated against them. But warm and loving nannies, such as Winston Churchill's Nanny Everest, did exist and did, to some degree, compensate for maternal deficiencies.

The nanny of American novelist Edith Wharton was of this loving breed, and she earned the undying affection of her

charge. A major contention here is that Nanny Doyley's presence shifted the forces within young Edith's family constellation and thereby modified her inner life. Biographers are
quick to fault Wharton's mother but insufficiently appreciative of the way the introduction of another woman into the
child's affections at a particularly sensitive stage could modify family relationships.

For a girl of Edith Wharton's time and social class, rearing
by nannies and governesses was customary. In old New York
society of the Gilded Age, socially prominent women like her
mother did not attend to the details of raising children, and
they were not negligent for hiring substitutes. They perceived their principal responsibility as maintaining the social position of the family by entertaining, making social
calls, appearing at cultural and charitable events, and being
generally ornamental. The daily care and training of children
they deemed fit occupation for working-class women with
genteel manners. Placing greater emphasis on the social aspects of the wifely role than on the nurturing function of
motherhood, they did not give much thought to the psychological impact of class differences between themselves and
their children's caretakers.

The meaning of such a widespread and accepted practice
differs according to the temperaments and circumstances of
children brought up under it. The differences lie in the specif-
ics of the individual life—the details of family relationships,
gender, class, culture, and most important, the degree and
direction of the child's responsiveness. I suggest here not that
surrogate nurturance is a negative practice with predictable
or measurable consequences, but merely that it is likely to
make some difference in the child's inner world. Rather than
try to judge whether the difference is detrimental or beneficial, I am inquiring in this case about a particular child's
sensitivity to such a practice and about the nature of her
adaptive mechanisms. In this book I study the effects of surrogate mothering on an extremely intelligent and reactive child

whose writings as an adult indicate that this experience was for her a formative one.

♦   ♦   ♦

My views on the subject of multiple mothering challenge those who believe that our tradition of mothers rearing their own infants is only a social construct, either an artifact of human history or part of a patriarchal plot to subjugate women. Following the lead of early twentieth-century thinkers such as Charlotte Perkins Gilman,[2] some feminists, including Dorothy Dinnerstein and Nancy Chodorow, among others, see nothing essential in the mother-child bond and believe that mothering can be done equally well by a father, an au pair, or the staff of a day-care center. According to this view, "'mother' is not a noun, it's a verb." Nancy Chodorow argues:

> The cross-cultural evidence ties women to primary parenting because of their lactation and pregnancy functions, and not because of instinctual nurturance beyond these functions. This evidence also suggests that there can be a variety of other participants in child care. . . . The prehistoric reasons of species or group survival which tied women to children have not held for centuries and certainly no longer hold today. . . . There is substantial evidence that nonbiological mothers, children, and men can parent just as adequately as biological mothers and can feel just as nurturant.[3]

This may well be true under certain circumstances, especially if the surrogate care is good and the mother would prefer to be doing something else. Today even mothers who long to tend their own infants are being driven into the work force in unprecedented numbers by economic pressures, earnestly hoping that their child-care arrangements will entail no loss to their babies.

In general, however, recent infant research stresses the exquisitely fine attunement between an infant and its biological mother. This begins during the long months of gestation that heighten the mother's awareness of the coming infant. Her interest is focused on this one as-yet unknown being, so that when it is finally revealed to her, she is attentive to its slightest signals. The focused attention generated during gestation and the early period just after birth is a major part of her message of care. According to research summarized by Joseph Lichtenberg, "Mothering behavior is primed for the immediate postpartum period and . . . early separation can adversely affect the developing maternal bond." He cites experiments showing a direct correlation between the amount of immediate mother-infant contact and the strength of the mother's bond to the child.[4]

Correspondingly, from its earliest days the child knows its mother from all other women—knows the contours of her face, the smell of her milk and her body, the sound of her voice—and prefers this woman to all others.[5] Ideally, each recognizes the other and validates the role of the other—the mother as a good mother, the child as an infant pleasing to this mother and safe in her care.

As D. W. Winnicott made us aware, the details of child care—from the manner of holding, feeding, and cleansing to attunement to the child's slightest signals—function as a language to which the infant responds in minutely sensitive ways. Through this mother-infant dialogue the child becomes socialized into a specific kind of human being. In this mutual attunement is the child's first experience of a shared world, an intersubjectivity that evolves into a need for sharing experience with others. On this first wordless dialogue rests the capacity for intimacy and a preference for certain kinds of relationships.[6]

The inherited range of potential selves becomes, through this interaction, a specific self with its own style of being in the world, its own style of loving, doing, and perceiving. Other primary caretakers would shape a different self because their language of behaviors and style of attunement would evoke different elements from the child's innate repertoire. Infants are adaptable and can shape a coherent self from a multitude of possible caretakers, but the current consensus indicates that lack of consistency and reliability in the first attachment can hinder development of a coherent self.

Even though a good surrogate is probably better for a child than a deficient mother, substitution of the first attachment figure with another (however capable and loving) initiates an obscure sense of deprivation, loss, and anger. A delicate link is violated, even though other, stronger ones may be forged. To regard as abandonment the commonplace practice of delegating a child's care to a professional caretaker may seem extreme, but the infant may experience it as abandonment and come to resent the mother of whose smell, voice, and hovering face it feels deprived. In cases described by psychoanalyst Harry Hardin, the child becomes estranged from its mother and perceives her as having turned away her face, or having turned her back to it.[7] Although quite capable of forming bonds with caretakers other than its biological mother, the child will retain in its soul this early bifurcation. A special and very refractory variety of psychic splitting will have occurred.

In discussing the strong attachment to mothers even of children who spend five days a week in day-care centers, from as early an age as three and a half months, psychoanalyst Louise J. Kaplan cites a study by Jerome Kagan of the maternal attachments of children raised communally on a kibbutz: "The number of hours a child is cared for by an adult is not the critical dimension that produces a strong attachment. There is something special about the mother-infant relationship. The parent appears to be more salient than substitute caretakers to the child. It is not clear why this is so."[8] The salience of birth mothers over "psychological mothers" even when there is no significant class difference testifies to the power of the biological bond but fails to address the consequences of severing the two.

If the caretaker is the one whose hands provide the closest experience of human contact, the one who really trains and socializes the child, the more salient mother, for whom the child's heart yearns, comes to seem rejecting and remote. Anger then taints this first love, and the child will have difficulty gaining a realistic image of its resented mother. The salient figure is not obliterated by the nanny; she holds her important place, but with her back turned, so to speak. A passage from Wharton's memoir quoted in the next chapter depicts her nanny and furry dog in the foreground of her family memories, her mother in the background with "all the dim, impersonal attributes of a Mother, without, as yet anything much more definite" (*Backward Glance*, 26).

Wharton regarded her nanny as a benevolent goddess who wrapped her in a cocoon of safety, but even good care proffered by a nursemaid is a commodity purchased by parents who renounce this role for themselves. Any nanny can be dismissed, and even if retained, she will depart eventually to care for other, younger children. When she leaves, the child feels abandoned, or, we might say, doubly abandoned, because the second loss amplifies the first. The child loses the illusion of what it never really possessed, an inviolable bond with its first beloved caretaker. The departure of a nanny seems a far more radical infidelity than the diversion of a mother's attention by a new baby; the nanny's total and seemingly willful disappearance must feel like a radical betrayal of love and trust.

Harry Hardin has studied the sequelae of early primary surrogate mothering in general and in the life of Sigmund Freud in particular. From his review of the scanty literature on the subject he concludes that those who experience nanny rearing tend to feel estranged from their birth mothers, that "surrogate mothering is synonymous with loss"[9] and usually results in problems with intimacy:

> Initially, introduction of a surrogate into the family may cause a severe disruption of the infant's relationship with his own mother; this occurrence may initiate the patient's life-long avoidance of further intimacy. Then, with rare exceptions, the infant inevitably, and often suddenly, loses the [surrogate] caretaker.... In my view, no infant can be psychologically unscathed by such trauma which so often occurs during its vulnerable separation-individuation phase of development.[10]

Furthermore, "as a result of her alienation, the mother is rendered incapable of adapting to her infant's changing requirements when the surrogate leaves."[11] Hardin adduces a case in which an infant perceived its return to the care of its natural mother as an adoption. Both mother and child, then, are altered by the introduction of an alternate primary care-taker.

The infant's attachment to a nanny is likely to cause the mother to become jealous. Loss of importance to her child acts as a negative reinforcement, reducing her pleasure in being a mother and creating friction within the triad. Without positive reinforcement, she will be less effective in her role. What is basically hers alone, the thrill of being the most important person in the world to this tiny, totally dependent human being, goes to a stranger. And eventually the child will feel guilt at having transferred this irreplaceable gift outside the family, where it will be lost forever, severed from its natural affective chain.

Probably Freud was the first to attempt a biographical inquiry into the psychic consequences of multiple mothering in his *Leonardo da Vinci and a Memory of His Childhood*. From the fact that Leonardo experienced dual mothers, a biological mother and an adoptive one, Freud derived the very shape and character of Leonardo's artistic and intellectual career as well as his sexual orientation. As many have recognized, Freud found and depicted in the pattern of Leonardo's childhood and career important features of his own development. His argument may have been weakened by scarcity of biographical data and an excess of interpretive zeal, but his method, if used cautiously, still offers us a useful model.

Powerful first-hand testimony about the mother-nursemaid split in the American South comes from novelist Lillian Smith in *Killers of the Dream*. After speaking nostalgically about the body of her own black mammy, she presents the personal and social consequences of the dual mother split:

> But this dual relationship which so many white southerners have had with two mothers, one white and one colored and

each of a different culture that centered in different human values, makes the Oedipus complex seem by comparison almost a simple adjustment.

Before the ego had gained strength, just as he is reaching out to make his first ties with the human family, this small white child learns to love both mother and nurse; he is never certain which he loves better. Sometimes, secretly, it is his "colored mother" who meets his infantile needs more completely, for his "white mother" is busy with her social life or her older children or perhaps a new one, and cannot give him the time and concern he hungers for. Yet before he knows words, he dimly perceives that his white mother has priority over his colored mother, that somehow he "belongs" to her, though he may stay more with the other. . . . His colored mother meets his immediate needs as he hungers to have them met. She is easy, permissive, less afraid of simple earthy biological needs and manifestations. When naughtiness must be punished, it is not hers but the white mother's prerogative to do so; and afterward, little white child runs back to colored mother . . . who soothes him. . . .

And now curious things happen. Strong bonds begin to grow . . . holding him to two women whose paths will take them far from each other. . . . His conscience, as it grows in him, ties its allegiance to [his white mother] and to the white culture and authority which she and his father represent. But to colored mother, persuasive in her relaxed attitude toward "sin," easy and warm in her physical ministrations . . . he ties his pleasure feelings. . . . A separation has begun, a crack that extends deep into his personality. . . . His "white" conscience, now, is hacking at his early love life, splitting it off more and more sharply into [polarities like mother and nurse, madonna and whore, pure and impure, conscience and pleasure, marriage and lust].[12]

This passage expresses dramatically the feeling of being split between two primary loyalties. Whether or not Lillian Smith's portrayal of the moral tone of black mammies is objectively true, she expresses the meaning for a child of the class difference between its two mothers.

Beyond the personality and mothering instincts of the two women lies the caretaker's embeddedness in a specific cultural tradition. Erik Erikson's studies of the way various cultural systems are encoded in traditional child-care practices depict the transmission of systems of value and behavior through the minutiae of the child-caretaker interaction. Ideally, caretakers' behavior conveys "a firm sense of personal trustworthiness within the trusted framework of their community's life style. . . . [Primary caretakers] must also be able to represent to the child a deep, almost somatic conviction that there is a meaning in what they are doing."[13] Should the meanings shift between two caretakers representing different cultural traditions, there is a risk of some flaw, however minute, in the development of basic trust.

Real-life experience of divided mothering appears to alter the functioning of the intrapsychic "good mother–bad mother" split described by object relations theory. For many of those who experience divided mothering, the gentle nurturing qualities cluster permanently around one of the two mother figures and the dangerous or threatening qualities around the other. The split contributes to a polarization of female attributes such that the two do not fuse in adulthood into a single realistic image of the mother as a whole woman comprising both positive and negative attributes. Integration into a single figure is necessary if the son or daughter is to be freed from domination by internalized mothers. As background for this study of Edith Wharton, I have examined the split-mother phenomenon in a variety of writers, not all of whom will be discussed here, and found in each instance significant consequences of that early experience. Among them are Sigmund Freud and his daughter Anna, William Faulkner, Edgar Allan Poe, Lillian Smith, Ellen Glasgow, and Honoré de Balzac.

Of course, the consequences vary according to countless circumstances such as personality, gender, social class, and the age of the child when the nursemaid enters its life. Research into the psychology of creativity, such as that by John Gedo, suggests that "children destined for greatness" are particularly sensitive to the presence or absence of parental support.[14] The earlier in infancy the surrogate situation is established, the more marked are the consequences. As an infant,

Balzac lived in the home of his peasant wet nurse, to whom he was so powerfully attached that he was furious at being returned to his mother after weaning. He never forgave his mother for abandoning him to the nurse in the first place or for removing him from her in the second.

But even when the nursemaid is not present from the beginning, the child's attachment can be very deep. Biographers attest to the importance of a black mammy in the life and work of William Faulkner. Although scholars differ as to whether Mammy Callie was present from his infancy or entered his life when he was five, his personality and fiction indicate a deep split in his maternal imagery that can be attributed to this divided love. As Judith Sensibar observes in analyzing what she considers an early screen memory, two cousins stand for two contrasting mother-figures, the biological mother and the mammy.

> [Cousin Vannye's] honey-colored hair looks inviting and seductive although she acts aloof and impersonal. But it is his other mother, the quick, dark Natalie (Caroline "Callie" Barr, his black nurse who cared for and lived with him from his birth until her death in 1940), who touches him and carries him. She offers him warmth and protection from "loneliness" and "sorrow."[15]

William Faulkner came to regard himself as one of his Mammy Callie's "white children" (the term he had inscribed on the tombstone he ordered for her). She was buried from his home, where, according to biographer Frederick Karl, she had been a "complete member of the household, beloved [and] respected."[16] Faulkner wrote to a friend:

> She still remained one of my earliest recollections, not only as a person, but as a fount of authority over my conduct and of security for my physical welfare, and of constant affection and love. She was an active and constant precept for decent behavior. From her I learned to tell the truth, to refrain from waste, to be considerate of the weak and respectful to age.[17]

The experiences of Sigmund Freud and his daughter Anna illustrate the patterns and variations I have found in the lives of creative personalities who had multiple mothering from early infancy. Unlike Leonardo, Freud had his two mothers simultaneously, not sequentially, and both of them within the important first years of life. Freud's young, inexperienced Jewish mother turned over to a middle-aged Catholic servant woman the major care of this precocious and highly responsive child.[18] His letters to Wilhelm Fliess attest to the nursemaid's crucial role in the formation of many of Freud's personality traits and—even more important—to her significance in the formation of his most influential theories. As I show in a study now in preparation, the infant Sigmund's experience of primary nurturing divided between mother and nanny caused a corresponding division in his female imagery, so that all the earthy and seductive qualities adhered to his nursemaid and the idealized ones to his mother. In turn, this split helped shape his major theories—his paradigms of family relationships and his attitudes toward women—and helped prepare his mind for formulation of the oedipal theory.

His daughter Anna could be said to have had *three* mothers—Martha Freud, her birth mother; Martha's sister Minna, who lived with the family and shared household responsibilities; and a *Kinderfrau* named Josefine, a Catholic nursemaid who was brought into the family at Anna's birth and remained until the girl started school. Although Josefine cared for the older children as well, Anna was her main responsibility. Josefine was her "primary caretaker" and became what Anna Freud herself called her "psychological mother." Anna's tribute to Josefine underscores what I consider the prototypical pattern in mother-nanny splittings: adoration of the nanny at the expense of the mother. She called Josefine "Meine alte Kinderfrau, meine alteste Beziehung und die allerwircklichste aus meiner Kinderzeit" ("my old nursemaid, my oldest relation, and the most genuine of my childhood").[19] For a person outside the family to be deemed the "most genuine relation" of someone's childhood is a phenomenon deserving very serious attention.

Anna enjoyed the ideal situation of every nanny-reared

child. She was Josefine's undisputed favorite. After a gas explosion in the Freuds' apartment, Josefine first rescued Anna and then returned to see about the other children. When asked by the brothers, "'If there were a fire, who would you save first?' . . . she answered unhesitatingly, 'Anna' . . . and it constituted proof of what [Anna] felt: that she was Josefine's favorite, Josefine's—in effect—only child." Anna reciprocated the preference. While in a park with her mother and Josefine, she lost sight of the nursemaid and ran off desperately to find her, getting herself lost in the process. Says Elisabeth Young-Bruehl of this event, "Many years later, Anna Freud used this story to indicate that it was Josefine's attention that made her feel secure."[20]

With her mother, Anna Freud at best maintained an armed truce, according to the evidence marshaled in Young-Bruehl's recent biography. Anna found Martha Freud too controlling and excessively involved in conventional domestic details and appearances and suffered under Martha's disparaging views of Anna's appearance and clothes. Clearly, Anna vied with mother and Tante Minna for the position of companion, aide, and later caretaker to Sigmund Freud. Always jealous of her mother and succeeding to an unusual degree in gaining possession of her father, she seems never to have seriously considered marriage.

Throughout her life, Anna Freud sought in close ties with women the love she had experienced with her old *Kinderfrau*. Some of these women were professional mentors, others intimate companions. Finding that many of Anna Freud's female attachments were attempts to recover her lost relationship to Josefine, Young-Bruehl writes of the tie to Lou Andreas-Salomé, "the childless Frau Lou had entered into the line of succession to Anna Freud's good mother, the adoring *Kinderfrau*, Josefine, for whom she had been an only child."[21]

With a Catholic nursemaid and a multiplicity of mother figures, Anna Freud's family constellation resembled that of her father. But the pattern of her personality shows remarkable analogies to that of Edith Wharton. Both women felt superior to their mothers and identified with and were mark-edly attached to their fathers. Anna Freud actually succeeded to an extraordinary degree in displacing her mother as her father's helpmeet. Freud's pun on his favorite daughter's name, "Anna Antigone," points frankly to the oedipal char-acter of their relationship. Edith Wharton's self-narrative con-nects the birth of her femininity and her literary gifts to the highly romanticized figure of her father. As a child she was acutely sensitized to whatever erotic signals emanated from that beloved man. What she may have made of such messages will be discussed in the next chapter.

Both women grew up feeling themselves to be physically unattractive, although they expressed their discomfiture in different ways. Edith Wharton tried to compensate with splen-did clothes; Anna Freud gave up competition and dressed inconspicuously. Both were the youngest children in their families and were so eager to catch up with the older ones that they scorned children's books in favor of adult stories about "true" life. Both very early expressed their fantasy lives in literary inventions, wrote highly personal poetry, and were strongly cathected to material adjuncts of the written word, Edith Wharton to certain books, Anna Freud to pens and other writing implements.

As powerful professional women, both experienced prob-lems in gender identity (what Anna Freud called a "masculin-ity complex") and struggled to accommodate both their ambi-tions and their need to give and receive nurturance. In their imaginative writings, both tended to identify with male char-acters. Both felt that their professional selves were masculine. They acted in the world as if they were males but expressed their maternal impulses in altruistic endeavors, such as car-ing for children displaced by war. Both were extravagantly fond of pet dogs; Wharton was rarely seen without at least one, and usually two, small lapdogs. Edith Wharton occasion-ally developed emotional attachments to children of her friends but, of course, did not make children her life work. Books were to be her offspring.

Most salient for our purpose here is the fact that both women adored their nannies and disparaged their mothers. And both, throughout life, sought various surrogates for their nannies, their lost "good mothers." Anna Freud found them in friends, colleagues, and mentors—members of her own social class. Although Edith Wharton had some women friends from her own milieu, she was emotionally dependent on a few servant women whom she kept close to her throughout life. With members of her own class, Wharton was a powerful and dominant figure, but her lifelong need for nurturance and dependency could best be met by working-class women. When the last of her beloved servants died she felt truly abandoned.

With Wharton as with many others, a loving mother surrogate somewhat ameliorated the consequences of maternal deprivation but did not fully compensate for it. Apparently a child's instinctive sensitivity to social class and power relationships tells it that the nursemaid, really a servant of the mother, lacks domestic and social authority. Wharton's memoirs and fiction tell us more or less directly that love without power within the child's own destined social world does not suffice to make it feel protected and prepared for life.

1

Family Ties

"M'ama . . . non m'ama . . . ," the prima donna sang,
and "M'ama!," with a final burst of love triumphant.
The Age of Innocence

Although Edith Wharton was endowed by nature with good
health and an appetite for sensuous experience, she suffered
in youth a repression of her sexuality so massive that she
claims to have known virtually nothing of the "process of
generation till [she] had been married for several weeks"
("Life and I," 33–34).[1]

Her marriage to Edward Wharton was virtually celibate
after this unfortunate beginning, so that her real sexual awakening was delayed until her mid-forties when she met and fell
passionately in love with Morton Fullerton. She attributed her
delayed sexual maturation and its attendant consequences to
her mother's prudish exaggeration of the Victorian sexual
code. Her childhood experiences served to magnify what social
historian Peter Gay calls the "learned ignorance" about sexual
matters imposed on women of Edith Wharton's time and class,
the Gilded Age of old New York society.[2] Her socially prominent
parents, George Frederic Jones and Lucretia Stevens Rhinelander Jones, epitomized the conservative values of that
society.

Wharton's depiction of the cult of female purity in *The Age
of Innocence* reveals that women knew how to work within
that convention, to maintain the appearance of innocence

while knowing well enough the important facts of life. In the words of May Welland, the incarnation of "factitious purity," "You mustn't think that a girl knows as little as her parents imagine. One hears and one notices—one has one's feelings and ideas" (149). Created in the author's late maturity, May Welland was granted a sophistication about sexuality that Wharton herself had lacked during her nubile years and was to acquire very painfully later in life. To a greater degree than others, the youthful Edith Wharton accepted the cultural fiction of female innocence and imposed it all too rigidly on herself.

She opens *The Age of Innocence* with Newland Archer entering his opera box in the midst of a performance of Gounod's *Faust* on the eve of his engagement, as Marguerite is singing "M'ama . . . non m'ama! . . . M'ama" ("He loves me, he loves me not, he loves me"). The words highlighted by this dramatic moment suggest a bilingual pun connecting love and mother, a pun derived from Edith Wharton's earliest affective life— mama, no mama, yet, after all, mama. Having a bodily mother whom she felt was no mother to her spirit, receiving compensatory love from a nanny, but having no single figure who reliably embodied the mothering function, young Edith had no mama, had two mamas, yet after all had one real mama who, by virtue of occupying the maternal space, exercised a powerful psychic sway. And the simultaneous having and not having of a mother contributed to difficulties throughout her affective life, so that when young she repressed all knowledge of sexuality, when married she lived celibate, and when she finally achieved sexuality in a midlife romance, she loved under adulterous and humiliating circumstances.

MOTHER AND NANNY

The division that Edith Wharton experienced between the biological and the nurturant aspects of mothering resulted in a general tendency to psychic splitting that was to permeate her feeling, her thinking, and eventually the very texture of her fiction. Nurturing, she tells us, came not from her socially preoccupied mother, but from a very devoted nanny. The contrast between the nanny's loving behavior and her mother's remoteness and judgmental attitudes magnified the normal intra-psychic split of good and bad mother.

The split that relegated to Lucretia Jones only the negative aspects of mothering—domination, intrusiveness, power to injure—created a pattern that would dominate Edith Wharton's psychic life and extend even beyond her mother's death. Once Lucretia Jones was cast into the role of the bad mother and became thus inscribed in her daughter's imagination, rectification of the mother-daughter relationship seemed almost impossible. The longevity of Wharton's anger is shown by her selection of illustrations for her memoir, *A Backward Glance*, which was written in her seventies, decades after Lucretia's death; she chose pictures of herself at various ages, several pictures of her houses, and portraits of her father, grandparents and great-grandparents and Henry James, but not a single image of her husband or her mother. The frightened child developed into an adult who spent considerable energy negotiating with her mother's influence, an adult who eventually achieved autonomy, but only at great cost.[3]

◆   ◆   ◆

Outwardly, Edith Wharton's childhood situation was not exceptional for a girl of her class and time. She was born in 1862 into a socially prominent New York family that was "well-off, but not rich" if compared to such magnates as the Astors, to whom they were related through the Schmermerhorns.[4] The family of George Frederic and Lucretia Jones lived comfortably on money derived from municipal real estate, which allowed them a fashionable existence in New York and Newport until post–Civil War inflation forced them to economize by living for many years in Europe, starting when Edith was four. Being a quick learner and voracious for knowledge, she

acquired fluency in the major European languages and a taste
for continental scenes, architecture, and culture. Building on
this base, she would later educate herself in languages, philosophy, religion, and literature, well beyond the accomplish-
ments of most women of her time.

After the family returned to America in Edith's tenth
year, she enjoyed the social life of both New York City and
Newport—nannies, governesses (but little formal schooling),
parties, and a fashionable debut. Altogether, she had a masterful intellect, social position, sufficient wealth to lead a fashionable life, and a privileged variety of experiences. Her memoir,
A Backward Glance, claims that her "little-girl life, safe,
guarded, monotonous, was cradled in the only world about
which, according to Goethe, it is impossible to write poetry"
(7), that is, an environment so satisfying that it provides insufficient conflict to inspire an artist.[5]

But social and family conditions were not nearly so bland
or so favorable as Wharton indicated. In "Life and I," an earlier and more candid manuscript version of her memoir, she
reveals that she had felt neither cradled nor safe. For her,
childhood was a series of terrors. She was worried, frightened, and subject to terrifying fears and compulsions. She
suffered from wide emotional swings ranging from helplessness to grandiosity, felt divided between incompatible public
and private selves, and was driven to extravagant and sometimes socially unacceptable activities.

By her own account, she suffered serious neurotic disturbances. She was afraid of animals other than small furry ones.
Frequently she experienced terrifying panic attacks while
waiting on the threshold of her parents' home, as if expecting
that the door might be opened by a witch. She dreaded all
tales of the supernatural, especially fairy tales, which feature
good and bad mother figures—fairy godmothers, stepmoth-
ers, and witches.[6]

These fears were later converted into psychosomatic or
neurasthenic illnesses, such as extreme reactions to minor

differences in temperature, nausea, anorexia, and asthma. In 1908 she wrote to Sara Norton:

> Tell Lily . . . that for *twelve years* I seldom knew what it was to be, for more than an hour or two of the twenty-four, without an intense feeling of nausea, and such unutterable fatigue that when I got up I was always more tired than when I lay down. This form of neurasthenia consumed the best years of my youth, and left, in some sort, an irreparable shade on my life. . . . I worked through it, and came out on the other side, and so will she.[7]

Wharton's agonizing symptoms conform remarkably well to those of the nineteenth-century neurasthenic woman as described by Elaine Showalter in *The Female Malady*. Although similar in many ways to hysteria, neurasthenia was considered a more "prestigious and attractive form of female nervousness than hysteria," comprising blushing, vertigo, headaches, neuralgia, insomnia, depression, and uterine irritability. With symptoms similar to those of hysterics, neurasthenics were thought to be more cooperative than hysterics, more ladylike and well-bred, more refined, and often more intellectually gifted and ambitious.[8] Neurasthenia like Wharton's was thought to result from sexual repression and other denials of bodily appetites in order to conform to a ladylike ideal, as well as to conflicts about "women's ambitions for intellectual, social, and financial success."[9]

Such pressures were particularly troublesome in Wharton's social milieu, which, in addition to fostering a repressive code of female behavior, distrusted intellectual ambition in general. Unlike Henry James, Wharton was born into the fashionable rather than the intellectual branch of the *haute bourgeoisie*, so that while living in America she had little contact with artists or literary people. As her friend Mrs. Winthrop Chanler put it: "The Four Hundred would have fled in a body from a poet, a painter, a musician or a clever Frenchman."[10] The part of Edith Wharton that identified with the values of her social set became uneasy about the artist and intellectual that was emerging from within, causing her to cultivate that artistic self in secret. Confused and lacking support for her emergent self, she rigidified the socially validated self into a virtual parody of the proprieties. Said a Newport acquaintance from the intellectual set, "Our acquaintance was slight, she belonging to the ultra-fashionable crowd, and I in quite another group. Though the intellectuals and the fashionables met, they never quite fused. She was slender, graceful and icy cold, with an exceedingly aristocratic bearing."[11] The exaggerated quality of Edith Wharton's aristocratic demeanor was also related to fear of her mother's disapproval.

Wharton's memoirs point directly to disturbances in the mother-daughter relationship as the origin of her problems. She portrayed her mother as a beautiful, fashionable, narrowly conventional society woman of fairly trivial interests. At nineteen, after a fairly adventurous and partially secret courtship, Lucretia Rhinelander married Edith's father, twenty-three-year-old George Frederic Jones—handsome, well educated, and well-to-do—the typical New York gentleman of Wharton's stories.[12] After settling in Gramercy Park, the bride entertained frequently and lavishly, "taking her place among the most elegant young married women of her day" (*Backward Glance*, 18). Rumor has it that the expression "keeping up with the Joneses" derived from the grand social presence of Lucretia Rhinelander Jones.

But Lucretia's elegance was at least partly compensatory. Although she had grown up enjoying an aristocratic family position, by the time of her coming out the Rhinelanders were often short of funds. Lucretia had to attend her own debut in a home-made gown and ill-fitting second-hand slippers. With experiences vacillating between pride and humiliation, Lucretia felt so insecure that she needed to fortify herself with external signs of social position—rigid proprieties and an inexhaustible supply of splendid clothes from Paris. Said her daughter with empathic relief at Lucretia's eventual reputation as the best-dressed woman in New York, "At last the home-made tarlatans and the inherited satin shoes were avenged" (18). Despite this apparent triumph, Lucretia was unable to impart social confidence to her daughter, who also tended to fortify herself with lavish clothes.

The couple had two sons, Frederic and Henry, who were respectively sixteen and twelve years older than Edith, the only girl of the family. When Edith was born, her father was forty, her mother thirty-seven years old. Family patterns and relationships were well established by this time, putting Edith into a fairly isolated position with regard to her brothers and even to her mother, who probably had little interest in return-ing to childrearing after so long an interval. The mother seemed distant, self-involved, and probably by this time more attuned to the ways of men than to the needs of a small girl.

Wharton's autobiographical documents depict her mother as cold, reproving, and remote. Motherly comfort came only from Doyley, her nanny. Here is the constellation as depicted in *A Backward Glance:*

> Peopling the background of these earliest scenes there were the tall, splendid father who was always so kind, and whose strong arms lifted one so high, and held one so safely; and my mother, who wore such beautiful flounced dresses, . . . and all the other dim, impersonal attributes of a Mother, without, as yet any-thing much more definite; and two big brothers who were mostly away. . . . but in the foreground with Foxy [her dog] there was one rich all-permeating presence: Doyley—a nurse who has always been there, who is as established as the sky and as warm as the sun, who understands everything, feels everything, can arrange everything, and combines all the pow-ers of the Divinity with the compassion of a mortal heart like one's own! Doyley's presence was the warm cocoon in which my infancy lived safe and sheltered; the atmosphere without which I could not have breathed. It is thanks to Doyley that not one bitter memory, one uncomprehended injustice, darkened the days when the soul's flesh is so tender, and the remem-brance of wrongs so acute. (26)

In the foreground of this family picture stand a nursemaid and a furry dog—someone to love her and something to love! And just as Doyley was the forerunner of Wharton's beloved servant Catherine Gross, that furry dog was the first of many that were to follow Wharton throughout life. Edith Wharton was usually seen holding one or more small dogs, cradling them in her lap, or draping them over her shoulders. Despite the benign atmosphere of *A Backward Glance*, bitter memories and injustices did indeed survive, and some were recorded in her abandoned autobiography, "Life and I." There she gives quite a different picture—a poignant account of mother's failure to provide the warm cocoon and of the consequences of living without one.

In many expressions of Wharton's spirit these joys and deficits of her formative years were to be recapitulated—the arms of the knightly father, and two female divinities, one remote, impersonal, disapproving, and sometimes punitive, the other a sheltering cocoon with powers of divine comfort. The child felt herself subjected to supernaturally beneficent and maleficent powers that controlled her bodily sensations—temperature, shelter, and the very breath of life. This feeling was to accompany her throughout life, causing restlessness and dissatisfaction with any one place or set of circumstances. She was always on the move, seeking the right place to be.

Despite the elaborate social life Wharton was to maintain in both America and Europe, she felt lonely, and despite elegant dwellings on two continents, she rarely felt at home. As she says of her perpetually displaced character Lily Bart, "the being to whom no four walls mean any more than others is, at such hours, expatriate everywhere." Having been unable fully to possess the cocoon that Doyley spun around her, Edith Wharton repeatedly sought and furnished new homes, perpetually seeking patriation in a home that would contain all the warring elements of her personality.

Doyley's very virtues altered the balance of forces within the Jones family. She became a standard of comfort against which Lucretia Jones looked inadequate to her daughter. Responding with all her grateful love to Doyley's nurturance, young Edith must have failed to give Lucretia signals that would have stimulated her latent maternal impulses and elicited warmer responses. The child must also have felt guilt for failing to love her mother and feared some retribution for giving to an outsider the love properly belonging to a parent. A negative cycle was generated between mother and daughter, with the mother reacting to the child's rejection and the child allowing negative imagery to fill the sacred maternal space. Lucretia came to seem like the God of Calvinism—vigilant, omnipresent, and unappeasable. Edith experienced a monumental need to placate this mother, a need so powerful that she offered up her own sexuality on the altar of this angry deity.

Such a cycle generates its own dynamics. Edith's image of her mother as a terrifying omnipresent power rendered the actual mother inaccessible for emotional support and ineffective in transmitting a model of capable femininity. Rejecting her mother, Wharton willed herself to be unlike Lucretia Jones in important ways. She tried to emulate her mother's elegance but rejected her role as an adult sexual being and mother. This separation of ornamental beauty from adult female sexuality is the genesis of Wharton's most touching figure, the exquisite Lily Bart, who seeks a husband but unconsciously sabotages every incipient union. In general, Wharton characters who are fitted by nature to relish the pleasures of life but always undermine their own hopes are revenants of the ardent Edith Wharton, a "life-lover" who so managed her affairs as to frustrate her own urgent desire for love and sexual fulfillment.

Receiving most of her nurturance from a surrogate mother added a deep insecurity to Edith's young life. Although Doyley remained with the Jones family well beyond Edith's infancy, she must have had day's off when the child feared she might never return. Knowing that Doyley was a salaried employee, Edith must also have feared that she might be dismissed. Attachment to Doyley and her later surrogates did not compensate for the maternal deficit, mainly because even the divine Doyley did not and could not suffice to fill the maternal role. Young Edith's polarization of the two women attributed to the mother power without love, to the nanny love without power. With mother perceived sometimes as a dim, aloof figure, sometimes as a punitive deity, and with nanny adored as an all-loving but powerless angel, the child stood frozen between mutually canceling antitheses. As a remedial figure of Wharton's childhood, Nanny Doyley ameliorated the child's sense of maternal deprivation, but as a domestic servant without power in Wharton's destined social world, she lacked authority. A servant is not a mother, at least not while the real mother is present. Doyley's visibly subordinate position in the household prevented her from assuming full maternal powers in Edith's mind. Motherhood is more than comfort, it is power and social efficacy, attributes belonging to the biological mother—to the mistress of the house and wife of the father.

To elaborate Melanie Klein's imagery of the good and bad breast (which can be intensified when the split images derive from separate maternal figures), each extreme implies its opposite. Doyley's very goodness evoked her polar negation—a persecutory biological mother who is both wronged and wronging. Having hypostatized the rejected mother into a hostile force, a vengeful Fury, Edith consumed considerable energy in efforts at appeasement. The sacrifices she made to this image, sacrifices of sexual curiosity and denial of sexual impulses and all that followed from such repressions, served to increase her anger and thereby her guilt.

The persecuting image of Edith's mother as judgmental, forbidding, aloof yet omnipresent, may have been a projection of the child's need for punishment rather than an accurate description. To some degree, Lucretia Jones probably *was* self-centered and preoccupied, but Wharton's own memoirs contain evidence that her mother cared about her. The record is contradictory. Wharton reports her parents' concern when she came near death from typhoid fever at a German spa in her ninth year. In their despair the parents daringly secured advice from the czar's personal physician, who prescribed plunging the child into ice-cold baths. "At the suggestion my mother's courage failed her; but she wrapped me in wet sheets, and I was saved" (*Backward Glance*, 41).

Mother and daughter took frequent carriage rides and made social calls together. Although young Edith felt herself to be homely and awkward in comparison to her beautiful mother, Lucretia Jones commissioned many paintings and photographs of her daughter and displayed them prominently.[13] Lucretia not only supervised Edith's reading but paid scrupulous attention to her diction and usage. She denied her daughter writing paper, so that the child had to write on discarded wrapping paper, but bought her a prized volume of poetry for her birthday. Although she seemed not to encourage Edith's creative writing, she tried to jot down the child's improvised oral narrations and, as Edith discovered after Lucretia's death, even saved copies of the child's letters to aunts and other relatives ("Life and I," 15). What was probably the most misguided of her attempts to relate to her daughter was her publication of Edith's adolescent verses without the girl's knowledge or permission.[14] This intrusive violation of her daughter's privacy was probably intended to be a pleasing surprise.

Regardless of the historical truth about Lucretia Jones, the internalized mother was experienced as a persecutory figure.[15] Wharton wrote of having suffered "excruciating moral tortures" that seemed derived from her mother but were actually self-imposed. She recognized that her parents, nanny, and governesses really had not preached, scolded, or "evoked moral bogeys." Indeed, she found that her parents were "profoundly indifferent to the subtler problems of the consciousness. They had what might be called the code of worldly probity." Mother's rule was politeness, father's was kindness; and the only behavior they really condemned was ill breeding. They had not even treated lying as particularly naughty:

> *My compunction was entirely self-evolved.* . . . I had never been subjected to any severe moral discipline, or even to that religious instruction which develops self-scrutiny in many children. . . . I had, nevertheless, worked out of my inner mind a

rigid rule of absolute, unmitigated truth-telling, the least im-
perceptible deviation from which would inevitably be punished by the dark Power I knew as "God." Not content with
this, I had further evolved the principle that it was "naughty"
to say, or to think, anything about anyone that one could not,
without offense, avow to the person in question. ["Life and I,"
4–5; italics added]

Her moral suffering came from the conflict between her own
impossibly high standards of truth and her mother's "code of
worldly probity." The conflict was dramatized when she was
berated by her mother for expressing publicly her thought that
a certain elderly woman was as ugly as an old goat: "For years
afterward I was never free from the oppressive sense that I had
two absolutely inscrutable beings to please—God & my
mother—who, while ostensibly upholding the same principles
of behaviour, differed totally as to their application. And my
mother was the most inscrutable of the two" (6–7).

With this oppressive presence the daughter craved to be
reconciled. Through fiction she tried to imagine ways of freeing herself from guilt and from fear of her mother's punitive
rage. She needed to bring her good and bad mother-figures
into relationship—to fuse them into a single image of compe-
tent, authoritative, and reliable nurturance. She searched her
imagination to create a usable maternal presence that would
meet her unsatisfied infantile needs and also be capable of
leading her into full womanhood.

She juxtaposes to an account of her burgeoning sensuality
the anguish of being shamed by her mother for seeking sexual
enlightenment:

Life, real Life, was . . . humming in my blood, flushing my
cheeks and . . . running over me in vague tremors when I rode
my poney [sic] . . . or raced & danced & tumbled with "the
boys." And I didn't know—& if . . . I asked my mother "What
does it mean?" I was always told . . . "It's not nice to ask about
such things." . . . Once, when I was seven or eight, an older
cousin had told me that babies were not found in flowers, but
in people. This information had been given unsought, but as I
had been told by mamma that it was "not nice" to enquire into

such matters, I had a vague sense of contamination, & went immediately to confess my involuntary offense. I received a severe scolding, & was left with a penetrating sense of "not-niceness" which effectually kept me from pursuing my investigations farther; & this was literally all I knew of the processes of generation till I had been married for several weeks. . . .

A few days before my marriage, I was seized with such a dread of the whole dark mystery, that I summoned up courage to appeal to my mother, & begged her, with a heart beating to suffocation, to tell me "what being married was like." Her handsome face at once took on the look of icy disapproval which I most dreaded. "I never heard such a ridiculous question!" she said impatiently; & I felt at once how vulgar she thought me.

But in the extremity of my need I persisted. "I'm afraid Mamma—I want to know what will happen to me!"

The coldness of her expression deepened to disgust [and the question went unanswered]. . . . *I record this brief conversation, because the training of which it was the beautiful and logical conclusion did more than anything else to falsify & misdirect my whole life.* ("Life and I," 33–35; italics added)

The fear of being thought unclean appears to have driven out whatever sexual knowledge Edith had picked up through her friends, her experience, and her extensive reading. She would not allow herself even to *think* whatever her mother decreed to be "not nice." Believing that mother could monitor even her thoughts, she effectively banished sexual knowledge from her mind, even to the point of believing "that married people 'had' children because God saw the clergyman marrying them through the roof of the church!" (34). The illusion of maternal omniscience generated such exaggerated compliance, such extreme scrupulosity, that her entire sexual nature—feelings along with knowledge—were driven underground.

Riven by such conflicts, Edith Newbold Jones was so unprepared for her marriage in 1885 at the age of twenty-three that for the next twelve years she suffered depression, nausea, and headaches. In 1898, thirteen years after the wedding, she required several months of residential psychiatric treatment. Her account of her mother's refusal to impart any sexual information, even when implored for it on the eve of the wedding, is now a famous part of Wharton folklore. Even if true as reported, the kind of total ignorance that Edith professes must be attributed as much to her own repression as to her mother's prudery. I suspect that then, as now, few women first learned the "facts of life" from their mothers or required elementary instruction on the eve of their weddings. If M. Jeanne Peterson's study of Victorian gentlewomen is applicable to American women of Edith Wharton's class and generation, they "knew about sex and had levels of tolerance about sexual matters and sexual misbehavior that belie the Victorians' reputation for prudery."[16]

Edith certainly was exposed to the usual stimuli that arouse sexual inquiry. She had many friends, especially among the boys of her acquaintance, whom she much preferred to girls. Her earliest recorded memory is of a highly pleasurable kiss from a small boy cousin, and she had two older brothers. She records episodes of flirtatiousness, which must have generated some somatic awareness of sexuality. In "Life and I" she documents a very normal curiosity about the first acts of husbands with respect to their brides: "I confess to a weakness for 'the Lord of Burleigh,' based I think, on its documentary interest as a picture of love and marriage (Subjects which already interested me profoundly.) From this poem I drew the inference that a husband's first act after marriage was to give his wife a concert ('and a gentle consort made he')" (9).

Another childish verbal misunderstanding illuminates the nexus in the child's imagination of adulthood, sexuality, and guilt. She had pondered the similarity between the words "adult" and "adultery"—noting that "persons who had 'committed adultery' *had to pay higher rates in travelling* (probably as a punishment for their guilt), because I had seen somewhere . . . the notice, '*Adults* 50 cents, children 25 cents' " (10). These examples indicate that considerable mental energy had been devoted to sexual investigation, bearing out Freud's view that speculation about the sexual activities of parents is the origin of intellectual curiosity—our first important attempt to puzzle out the unknown. He surmised that children would divine the facts of generation even if never informed of them.[17]

Puberty and menstruation must have raised additional curiosity. After her early debut at seventeen, she joined a social circle of young married women, who must have communicated something of the realities of married life. If she really arrived at marriageable age believing that women become pregnant because God sees their weddings through the roof of the church, what prevented so intelligent a person from checking out this unlikely supposition?

Rather than join the general indignation against Lucretia Jones for her purported rejection of Edith's prenuptial questions about what happens to women when they marry, I am tempted to echo Lucretia's observation that Edith must have noticed that men and women are made differently, and that she "can hardly be as stupid as she pretends."[18] The not-quite-credible wedding eve story may reflect displaced anger at Lucretia Jones's astonishing omission of Edith's name from the invitations to her own wedding, which reads, "Mrs. George Frederic Jones requests the honor of your presence at the marriage of her daughter to Mr. Edward R. Wharton, at Trinity Chapel, on Wednesday April Twenty-ninth at twelve o'clock."[19]

Edith's request for sexual information could have masked a shy desire for intimacy with her mother—a sharing of womanly secrets. *The Old Maid*, Wharton's fictive treatment of such an interview on the eve of marriage, clearly points less toward sexual instruction than toward mother-daughter intimacy just before the daughter's entry into the married state. Imparting such information before a wedding may be a ritual designed to transmit female adulthood from mother to daughter, and this transmission is exactly what failed to occur in Edith Wharton's development.

THE "NO" OF THE MOTHER,
THE REALM OF THE FATHER

Wharton's conceptions of power, gender, and sexuality were
derived from the complex politics of her family constellation.
The partial displacement of Lucretia Jones by a nursemaid
affected Edith's sexual development by altering the dynamics
of the oedipal phase and making space in the child's psyche
for unusually florid incestuous fantasies. Lucretia's inability
to hold onto her own daughter's affection may have suggested
a similar slackness in her hold on her husband, leaving a
power gap into which the child's imagination might enter.
And, as I discuss more fully in Chapter 4, the split maternal
image might have suggested a fancy that her brother's tutor
and not George Frederic Jones was really her father, thus rendering Mr. Jones more available as an object of sexual fantasies. Given the extravagance of Edith's imagination and the
energy she put into sexual investigation, there are manifold
possibilities for elaboration of the forces within the family
system.

Balancing the two female figures of her childhood was the
"tall, splendid father who was always so kind, and whose
strong arms lifted one so high" (*Backward Glance*, 1), a figure
who, unlike the mother, was immune from the rancor of childhood disappointments. Edith idealized him and identified
with him. Married shortly after his graduation from Colum-
bia College, he inherited enough money that he never had to
work for a living. He lived a life of gentlemanly leisure, occupying himself largely with work on the boards of charitable
and cultural institutions.

The recollection of a proud childhood walk with him is the
opening note of *A Backward Glance*. In this radiant memory
Wharton found the formation of one aspect of her selfhood: "I
may date from that hour the birth of the conscious and feminine *me* in the little girl's vague soul" (2). With her father as
the mirror of her fine appearance, she came to experience

herself as a "subject for adornment." Her pride in being daddy's pretty little companion includes a romantic attachment to this handsome father, competition with her mother for this position, and a compassionate loyalty to him.

But as Adrienne Rich says, a nurturing father "must be loved at the mother's expense."[20] Edith saw her father as a fellow victim of Lucretia's materialism and social ambitions. During the Civil War years, the Jones income suffered from fluctuations in real-estate values, causing the family to spend about eight of Edith's childhood years in Europe to reduce expenses. Edith remembered her father bent over his desk in "desperate calculations . . . in the vain effort to squeeze my mother's expenditures into his narrowing income."[21] To this image of paternal worries she juxtaposed that of her mother as a "born shopper" who indulged in unnecessary buying until the money "gave out."

She tended to visualize her father in his library, a small room decorated in the Walter Scott tradition, with an oak mantelpiece "sustained by vizored knights." The room was "lined with low bookcases where, behind glass doors, languished the younger son's meager portion of a fine old family library."[22] This typically Victorian "gentleman's library" became Edith Wharton's schoolroom, her university, and her emotional center.

Beginning to sense her own mental powers, Edith turned to her father as the source of what she valued most in herself and to his library as the locus of her most valued experiences. With important consequences for her artistic persona, she came to regard him as the generator of her literary self. He taught her how to read and introduced her to poetry: "My first experience of rhyme was the hearing of the "Lays of Ancient Rome" read aloud by my father. . . . The metre was intoxicating" ("Life and I," 9).

She found or read into this mild, wife-dominated gentleman a love of poetry and a literary talent frustrated by his wife's prosaic values. She wrote, expressing great pity for his lost sensibilities:

The new Tennysonian rhythms also moved my father greatly; and I imagine there was a time when his rather rudimentary love of verse might have been developed had he had any one with whom to share it. But my mother's matter-of-factness must have shrivelled up any such buds of fancy . . . and I have wondered since what stifled cravings had once germinated in him, and what manner of man he was really meant to be. That he was a lonely one, haunted by something unexpressed and unattained, I am sure. (*Backward Glance*, 39)

The polarizing tendency described above with respect to the dual mother figures was also at work in Wharton's imagery of her two parents. She perceived them as negations of each other, with all the good directed toward the father. Onto him she projected her own sense of victimization by a female, so that Lucretia seemed to shrivel the soul of this sensitive man. Wharton's fiction frequently echoes this pattern of shy male sensibility sacrificed to female crassness.

Edith's father gave her the freedom of his library. Her mother read novels avidly but forbade them to the daughter because of their sexual content. Young Edith obeyed her mother's rule but used her library privilege to frustrate its intent. She must have been something of a casuist, evading the ban on novels by reading plays, the first that she recalls being about a prostitute. From her readings in the Bible, poetry, and Elizabethan drama she must have found all the clues she needed to surmise "the facts of generation," but feeling guilty about knowledge forbidden by her mother, managed to repress it. Lucretia Jones's prudery triumphed better than she knew or intended—Edith became distanced from her developing erotic feelings and transferred all her passion into the area of books and imagination.

She developed a rapturous relationship to the written word, to which her beloved father had introduced her. His library became a "secret garden," a locus of virtually ecstatic experiences, from the sensuous pleasures of luxurious bindings to those of the expanding imagination: "Whenever I try to recall my childhood it is in my father's library that it comes to life. I am squatting on the thick Turkey rug . . . dragging out book after book in a secret ecstasy of communion. . . . There was in me a secret retreat where I wished no one to intrude" (69–70; note the identification here of the library with her self or her body).

Activities connected with books, whether hearing stories read, making up her own stories, or browsing among the books, are described in "Life and I" in orgasmic language. She experienced a "sensuous rapture" from the spoken and written word even before she knew how to read. She tells of a "devastating passion" for the process of "making up," which consisted of pacing the floor holding a specific book (often upside-down) and ecstatically pouring out invented tales as if she were reading them. She managed to turn the pages at approximately the right intervals, hoping that the watching adults believed she could read. The rapture was tied to specific editions of specific books, so that "invention flagged unless I had the right print." She was under such urgent compulsion to repeat this activity that she would have to abandon playmates in order to relieve her tension at fairly frequent intervals.

> I used to struggle as long as I could against my perilous obsession, & then, when the "pull" became too strong, I would politely [ask mother to make my excuses because] "I must make up." And in another instant I would be shut up in her bedroom, & measuring the floor with rapid strides, while I poured out to my tattered Tauschnitz, the accumulated floods of my pent-up eloquence. Oh, the exquisite relief of those moments of escape from the effort of trying to "be like other children"! . . . I don't think I exaggerate or embellish in retrospect the ecstasy which transported my little body & soul when I shut myself in & caught up my precious Tauschnitz. ("Life and I," 12–13)

Even allowing for hyperbole, "making up," as she called it, sounds like what youngsters today call "making out." Young Edith would take the specific editions of books to which her rapture was cathected from her father's library to her mother's bedroom and then engage in this tension-relieving outburst of narrative. She needed to make her mother a witness to her narrative frenzies. The whole cluster of activities—the locales, and the sequence and language in which she reports them— suggest that some erotic arousal had occurred in her father's library, and that she felt her mother should be aware of it.

Edith's reading probably stimulated sexual fantasies and perhaps some autoerotic activity. Indeed, a survey of Wharton's fiction and poetry reveals what Candace Waid calls an "extravagant desire for knowledge," which in the poem "Vesalius in Zante" focuses on the female reproductive system. Both Vesalius and his successor Fallopius, whose anatomical research led him to discover the fallopian tubes, "rent the veil of flesh and forced a way / into the secret fortalice of life." In this dramatic monologue the living female body is troped as a book or scroll that the anatomist violates in his lust for knowledge. Vesalius defends thus his dissection of a still-living cataleptic girl:

> If my blade
> Once questioned living flesh, if once I tore
> The pages of the Book in opening it,
> See what the torn page yielded ere the light
> Had paled its buried characters—and judge![23]

As Waid observes, "the juxtaposition of wounding and violation with the problem of penetrating the secrets of the female body culminates in these poems with an epistemologically and sexually charged concern with the female organs of reproduction."[24] By imaging exploration of the secrets of the female body as the tearing open of a book, Wharton perhaps suggests the core fantasy or psychological nexus involved in her sexualization of books and libraries.

The eroticized images of the human hand that appear frequently in Wharton's work point in several directions. Some arise in connection with father figures, some with lovers, but they may also refer to autoerotic activity. The ecstatic poem "Life," published in 1908 and delirious with erotic excitement, is narrated by a water reed that has been ravished into expression by Life, an allegorical female figure. Life, exclaims the reed, "in my live flank dug a finger-hole, / and wrung new music from it." As player of the reedpipe, Life sets the pipe's flanks aquiver with ecstasy: "into my frail flanks / Into my bursting veins, the whole sea poured / Its spaces and its thunder."[25] A river reed played on by the hand and lips of a female figure and endowed with quivering flanks offers so many interpretive possibilities that one cannot confidently chart the metaphoric path. But the poem, with its multivalent eroticism and swift alternations of polarity, seems propelled by the flow between sexuality and creativity.

The hands that play the reedpipe in "Life" anticipate the role of hands in the incestuous "Beatrice Palmato" fragment that Wharton regarded as unpublishable (see Appendix). Hands are prominent not only in the name "Palmato" but in the fact that father-daughter incest had been carried on for years by means of mutual manual stimulation. The difference between the plot summary "Beatrice Palmato" and its appended "Unpublishable Fragment" illuminates the nature of Edith Wharton's preoccupation with incest. In the startlingly erotic, if not pornographic, depiction of incest in the "Fragment," a father and daughter joyously consummate shortly after the daughter's marriage the desire that had always permeated their relationship. This episode unfolds the incestuous implications concealed within the plot summary, while the summary supplies a familial frame for the "fragment."[26]

The summary presents the parents of Beatrice Palmato, her first name probably an allusion to Beatrice Cenci, the sixteenth-century Roman woman whose name has a long association with incest. Cenci joined a plot to assassinate her father for his "unnatural" acts. Her mother, interestingly enough, was named Lucrezia. Beatrice Palmato's mother was a shy, silent, emotionally troubled woman, and her father, the half-Levantine, half-Portuguese Palmato, was a wealthy, cultivated, and artistic London banker. In this family, affective lines run in an oedipal direction; the mother passionately favors her son, the father his daughters. Following the suicide of an older daughter for unspecified reasons, the mother suffers mental disturbances that require hospitalization, leaving Beatrice in the care of the father and a governess, whom the father marries after his wife's death in an insane asylum.

At age eighteen, the lively, brilliant, artistic Beatrice Palmato marries an amiable but dull country squire. Her friends are surprised at this match, as were Wharton's friends by her marriage to Teddy. Beatrice promptly loses her sparkle, slumping into a general depression, and brightens only during an extended trip to Paris with her father. Mr. Palmato dies uneventfully during Beatrice's twentieth year, the age at which Edith Wharton lost her father.

Beatrice bears two children and becomes morbidly jealous of her husband's affection for their daughter, a brilliant replica of herself. One day Beatrice grows furious at seeing her husband innocently kiss their little girl after a long absence. From this irrational outburst the husband suddenly recognizes "many mysterious things in their married life—the sense of some hidden power controlling her, and perpetually coming between them, and of some strange initiation, some profound moral perversion."[27] His recognition of her moral condition leads Beatrice to commit suicide. Only subsequently, in conversation with her brother, does the husband connect the obscure barrier in his marriage to Mr. Palmato, but the act of incest is left unspecified. With the horror implied but unstated, the summary has the makings of a powerful story, but Wharton never wrote it.

In the "Unpublishable Fragment" she unfolds the "perversion" in the life of Beatrice, depicting with exquisite relish the same horrific experiences that the plot summary barely suggests. Between these two documents we have two sides of an incest experience—the daughter's pleasure in bringing to climax a lifetime of paternal seduction, and the same woman's horror as she lives out the consequences of incestuous abuse and imagines her own daughter becoming a victim of it. By virtue of the dual perspective created by these separate versions, Wharton offers a private and a social vision of the same

act—secret pleasure for a limited period within the daughter's consciousness, but dire consequences when that daughter tries to move out of the enclosed relationship into the
social world of marriage and childrearing. For that outward
move, Beatrice has become permanently incapacitated.

Curiously, Mr. Palmato deferred the consummation of his
lust until a week after Beatrice had been deflowered by her
bridegroom. Then, in a scene of sensuous luxury, father and
daughter view each other's bodies for the first time. Wharton
makes it very clear that hitherto Mr. Palmato had been stimulating Beatrice with his hand; now, in order to advance to the
full sexual act, he brings her along by the established, familiar route. His hand "softly separated her legs, and began to
slip up the old path it had so often travelled in darkness." He
manipulates her genitals with his "subtle forefinger" and then
penetrates them with his tongue. Next he presses "into her
hand the strong fiery muscle that they used, in their old joke,
to call his third hand."[28]

The father exults in the idea that Beatrice's husband had
served only as gatekeeper to this moment, the consummation
of her true passion. He had felt that she would accept him
fully only after she has experienced the "eagerness bred of
privation . . . the dull misery of her marriage," a stage not
likely to have developed only a week after her wedding.[29] The
fragment concludes with genital intercourse, but only after
carefully establishing the pair's long-continued practice of
mutual masturbation.

Her bridal experiences, Mr. Palmato felt, would pale in comparison to what Beatrice's patient, imaginative, sexually accomplished father could offer. The particulars of Beatrice's
unsatisfying marriage are so loaded with references to Wharton's own marriage that some degree of autobiographical allusion is likely in the incestuous experiences as well, though
probably enhanced by the imagination of a woman long sexually deprived.

If, as seems plausible, young Edith had experienced some
kind of incestuous stimulation, we can more easily under-

stand her emotional volatility and overactive sense of guilt. Such an event would also have contributed to the astonishing repression of all sexual knowledge and years of sexual abstinence that we have already seen.[30] Her psychosomatic ailments and her protective attitude toward her father resemble the pattern of women who have been sexually abused in childhood. In general, such women tend either to become promiscuous or to fear sexuality and abjure sex altogether.[31] An incest victim's sense of personal degradation motivates the Palmato plot summary; her voluptuous fantasies generate the "unpublishable fragment."

The half-Portuguese, half-Levantine Palmato, leading a life of cultured leisure not unlike that of George Frederic Jones, would have been an alien in London society. "Portuguese" may signify "Continental" and, according to the cultural stereotype, sexually liberated, but "Levantine" unmistakably means Jewish. The fact that Wharton went out of her way to endow this father with exotic racial origins suggests the kind of taboo that Leslie Fiedler long ago identified as the projection of our unacceptable sexual desires onto a despised minority.[32] Although Wharton had some Jewish friends, including Bernard Berenson and Rosa Fitz-James, whom she must have regarded as exceptions, she shared the prejudices of her class and time and probably shared some of the projective tendencies as well. Her fictional references to Jews display the prevailing racial stereotypes, sometimes with an aura of erotic ambivalence.

Ambiguities in *The House of Mirth* regarding the character of Simon Rosedale, who is an object of disdain despite his many admirable traits, suggest that in Wharton's fiction Jews signify tabooed sexual attraction. She characterizes another Levantine, Ladislas Isador in *A Son at the Front* as a "clever, contriving devil" who is also a philanderer.

> Ladislas Isador killed at the front! The words remained unmeaning; by no effort could Campton relate them to the fat middle-aged philanderer with his Jewish eyes, his Slav eloquence, his Levantine gift for getting on, and for getting out from under. . . . What a mad world it was, in which the same

horrible and magnificent doom awaited the coward and the hero! (180)

Whether Jewish or not, the father-derived figures in Wharton's work act as forces inhibiting sexual consummation with more appropriate men. We notice, for example, that Simon Rosedale is virtually omniscient about Lily Bart's attachments to other men and always lets her know that he has seen or heard of each event. Similarly, in *The Age of Innocence* the implicitly Jewish financier Julius Beaufort, after interrupting almost every one of Newland Archer's visits to Countess Olenska, breaks into their incipient tryst in the patroon's house and thus short-circuits the fulfillment of their passion. In this significantly named house of the father, desire between Newland and Ellen may not be consummated. Like Rosedale, Beaufort appears to have uncanny knowledge of the lovers' sexual intentions. In Wharton's fiction, the omniscient figure who intervenes between lovers usually inhibits the sexual act, but not for moral reasons. He *comes between* desire and its consummation, suggesting that he himself is the true object of desire.

Wharton's emphasis in the first pages of *A Backward Glance* on "the large safe hollow of her father's hand" links incestuous motifs echoing through erotic scenes in her fiction to the possibility of sexual stimulation by her father. There is no sign of anything like the flagrant sexual abuse experienced by Virginia Woolf,[33] but Wharton's writings suggest that she might have experienced some variety or degree of seductive behavior. The case is at most circumstantial. If there was seductive behavior, it could well have been minor or ambiguous. Perhaps there was only some unintended contact or touching that was magnified by the decidedly inflammable imagination of the love-hungry daughter. Any kind of erotic exchange between Edith and her father would have provided yet another motive for rivalry with the mother, mixed with anger at her for not fulfilling her duty to maintain the boundary against incest.

"The House of the Dead Hand," written in 1898 and published in 1904, provides an early instance of the hand motif embedded in biographically relevant family symbolism.[34] The Lombard family lives in Siena with an old woman servant in a gloomy mansion that displays over its threshold a female hand carved in sallow marble, which seems to be the emblem of "some evil mystery within the house" (*Collected Stories*, 509). The family constellation allies father and daughter in artistic sensibility against the dull triviality and incomprehension of the mother.

Like Hawthorne's "Rappaccini's Daughter," this Italian tale presents a father who coopts his daughter's sexuality and subordinates her freedom to his own lust for knowledge. Sounding a bit like Wharton's Fallopius, Dr. Lombard boasts that he has "violated the tomb" of the Renaissance, "laid open its dead body, and traced the course of every muscle, bone and artery" (514). Dr. Lombard's entrapment of his daughter also echoes that of Dr. Sloper in Henry James's "Washington Square."

Dr. Lombard has induced his daughter Sybilla to purchase with the money intended for her dowry a Leonardo painting of a lascivious woman posed in front of a crucifixion. This sensuous painting, really Sybilla's property, has become her father's peculiar treasure. He, not his daughter, controls access to the picture, which is kept hidden in the depths of the house, shrouded from light by blinds and a velvet curtain. From a vantage point marked by a pomegranate bud in the carpet, he allows chosen visitors to view it on condition that they never reproduce it in any way. Because Sybilla's dowry is tied up in the painting that her obsessed father will not let her sell, she cannot marry the man she loves. Even after Dr. Lombard's death, she fails to seize the opportunity for which she had long plotted; she would never feel free to sell the hated picture or to marry. The rest of her adult life will be governed by the dead hand of her father: "I can't lock him out; I can never lock him out now" (529).

A father who cannot be locked out, who dominates his

daughter's personal treasure and forecloses her opportunities for marriage and reproductive life, surely suggests an incestuous relationship. But the fact that the marble hand above the threshold is a specifically female hand complicates the evil that it symbolizes. In contrast to her elderly father's vivacity, Sybilla seems passive, sullen, and lifeless, a little like the nineteenth-century depiction of masturbators, who ruin their health by expending vitality in a sexual dead-end. The dead hand over the threshold may have a dual significance—abuse of Sybilla by her father as well as self-abuse.

The story reeks with erotic symbolism such as dark corridors, the parting of velvet folds to reveal hidden treasure, a female image that can be contemplated but must never be reproduced. The hand symbol, however awkwardly presented, forms the center of an image constellation that is characteristic of Wharton's imagination—father-daughter relationships, fearful thresholds, lust for knowledge, and the often-recurring pomegranate.

◆   ◆   ◆

We do not know what occurred in George Frederic Jones's library, but given the conjunction of books, libraries, and compulsive outbursts of oral narration using certain books as fetishes, one may hypothesize the existence of a psychic nexus that embraced Wharton's creative as well as her erotic life. Books and even words became libidinized, the library became a place of secret initiation:

> But this increase of knowledge was as nought compared to the sensuous rapture produced by the sound & sight of the words. . . . They were visible, almost tangible presences, with faces as distinct as those of the presences among whom I lived. And, like the Erlkönig's daughters, they sang to me so bewitchingly that they almost lured me from the wholesome noonday air of childhood into the strange supernatural region where the normal pleasures of my age seemed as insipid as the fruits of the earth to Persephone after she had eaten of the Pomegranate seed. ("Life and I," 10)

The garnet-colored seeds, sown throughout Wharton's work from early to late (as the title of a Wharton story, a poem, and of works by her fictive writers such as Margaret Aubyn), mark the trail we have been trying to follow toward the center of this imagery complex. As Candace Waid pursues it in *Letters from the Underworld*, "'insipid' means tasteless, but it also suggests a lack of 'sapience' or wisdom. The pomegranate seed in contrast is among the forbidden fruits . . . associated with secret knowledge." Waid interprets Persephone's acceptance of her abduction into the dark realm of Pluto as rejection of her mother's "noonday fertility," an escape from that sunny but commonplace world.[35] But when we refer Persephone's dark knowledge of the underworld to Wharton's reading in Ovid's *Metamorphoses V*, the story may also be a commentary on a maiden's sudden ravishment into a marriage for which she was unprepared.

In Ovid's version, the childlike Persephone, who wishes to remain a virgin, is innocently gathering flowers when her uncle Pluto, struck by an arrow from Eros, suddenly abducts her. Her cries to her mother avail her nothing. Through a crevice in the earth, she is carried into the underworld by the captor who had never sought her consent. Had she abstained from food while in Hades, she might have returned to her mother. But the seven pomegranate seeds that she ate there allowed her only seasonal visits to the sunlit world of her mother, the goddess of fertility. Although pomegranates traditionally symbolize female fertility, in this story they also suggest the male seed of which Persephone had accepted only a little, but enough to prevent annulment of her marriage, so that for half the year she remains a prisoner in her husband's house.

Wharton might have heard many personal themes in the Persephone-Demeter story, perhaps different ones over the years in which she pondered it. The maiden rapt all unprepared into marriage recalls Wharton's account of the marriage she entered in apparent ignorance of "the facts of generation." Additionally, it could have reverberated to a certain reluctance on her part to accept the prescribed female destiny (the "marriage plot," as Carolyn Heilbrun describes it in *Writing A Woman's Life*), in order to retain the autonomy necessary for pursuing her own creative life. Having yielded to social expectations by marrying, she might unconsciously have resisted the wifely role by cultivating sexual ignorance and later by fleeing to illness as a kind of Eriksonian moratorium, a private space in which her few seeds might germinate.

In one of her most moving poems, "Pomegranate Seed" (1912), Wharton draws together two of her most pressing concerns—her failure to participate in the chain of generation, and the way that failure separates daughter from mother. Demeter longs for the opportunity to show her daughter the ways of life in the warm sunlight, for Persephone to observe how a woman should,

> Under the warm thatch, in the winnowing creel,
> Lay the New infant, seedling of some warm
> Noon dalliance in the golden granary,
> Who shall in turn rise, walk, and drive the plough,
> And in the mortal furrow leave his seed.[36]

But as wife to Pluto, Persephone nurses only "waxen-pale dead babes." Procreatively, Persephone is at a dead end, whereas the bereft Demeter is part of the continuity of life. But as Demeter says in parting, "Thou knowest more than I." Through an uncle's act of rapine, Persephone has acquired a kind of sexual knowledge that not only sets her above her mother, but sets her off from common human experience. Perhaps with a peculiar pride, Persephone comes to treasure this dark knowledge as the jewel of her uniqueness, so rare that it makes ordinary life seem insipid.

"Pomegranate Seed" suggests the powerful mother-daughter yearning to which Wharton might have responded in the Persephone story. Unlike Ovid's version, which is fairly balanced between mother and daughter, most of Wharton's dramatic narrative focuses on the desperation of Demeter, "undaughtered" by her loss. The powerful expression of mother love in this poem suggests that Wharton needed to imagine such a passion because she longed to be the recipient of it. In this way, she could experience herself as the loved daughter for whom Demeter so intensely searches.

Edith Wharton's very daunting task was to create an authorial self from the traumas and defenses of her childhood experience. Eventually she would be able to declare triumphantly, *"Gods of heaven & Gods of hell I saw face to face & adored them."*[37] But in the meantime, intellect, creativity, and secret erotic pleasure had become the realm of the father, bounded firmly by the "no" of the mother and therefore dissociated from the child's feminine self.

THE GENDER SPLIT

So extravagantly did this gifted child experience life that she had to develop her own mechanisms for keeping herself in equilibrium. Of her mental state she said,

> The picture I have drawn of myself . . . is that of a morbid, self-scrutinizing and unhappy child. I *was* that—and yet I was also, at the same time, a creature of shouts and laughter, of ceaseless physical activity, of little wholesome vanities and glowing girlish enthusiasms. And I was also—and this most of all—the rapt creature who heard the choiring of the spheres, and trembled with a sensuous ecstasy at the sight of beautiful objects, or the sound of noble verse. I was all this in one, and at once, because I was like Egmont's Clarchen, "now wildly exultant, now deeply downcast," and always tossed on the waves of a passionate inner life. I never felt anything *calmly*—and I never have to this day! ("Life and I," 41; Wharton's italics)

This extreme responsiveness resulted in a fear of being overwhelmed by intense experiences, causing her to limit her exposure to them, to live as she said, "on a reduced diet" and let her imagination supply the richness. Imagination seems to have provided for Wharton the deepest experience of reality. For this reason she may have derived her best nourishment from what Emily Dickinson called "a banquet of abstemious-

ness." Wharton's description of what she made imaginatively
of scarce and forbidden material offers a clue to what may
have become her preferred style of experience. Having been
forbidden in youth by her mother ever again even to glance at
a "fashionable hetaera" who drove out in a canary-colored
carriage, she thereafter dutifully looked away

> when the forbidden brougham passed; but that one and only
> glimpse of the loveliness within it peopled my imagination
> with images of enchantment. . . . She was . . . my first doorway
> to romance, destined to become for me successively Guinevere
> and Francesca da Rimini, Beatrix Esmond and the *Dame aux
> Camélias.* And in the impoverished emotional atmosphere of
> old New York such a glimpse was like the mirage of palm trees
> in the desert.[38]

Tossed about on waves of feeling, young Edith was desperate for an ordering principle in her life and sought it in books.
Isolated as the last child in an already grown family of two
sons, she had come to feel that helplessness and bewilderment
were female traits and that logic, rationality, and control
were male. Viewing her childish ignorance of life as a girlish
limitation and wishing to understand the adult world of her
parents and brothers, she disdained children's books. Determined to find her own way out of being such a "helpless blun-
dering thing, a mere 'little girl' " ("Life and I," 33), she would
master chaos by means of philosophic books such as brother
Harry's college text, Coppée's *Elements of Logic.* She developed strategies for developing the "male" side of her personality to defend and protect the terrified female self. She cultivated rational, analytic skills, and acquired immense stores of
theoretical learning.

> I can only suppose it answered to some hidden need to order
> my thoughts, & get things into some kind of logical relation to
> each other: a need which developed in me almost as early as
> the desire to be kissed & thought pretty! It originated, perhaps,
> in the sense that weighed on my whole childhood—the sense of
> bewilderment, of the need of guidance, the longing to under-

stand *what it was all about*. My little corner of the cosmos seemed like a dark trackless region "where ignorant armies clash by night," & I was oppressed by the sense that I was too small & ignorant & alone ever to find my way about in it. ("Life and I," 27–28; Wharton's italics)

Pride in her analytic faculty, which she considered a masculine attribute distinguishable from her feminine gifts, was to remain with her throughout life. Percy Lubbock expressed the dichotomy as both Wharton and her acquaintances perceived it: "More than one of her friends have already noted, without surprise, that she preferred the company of men; and indeed there are some obvious reasons why she should, two of the more obvious being that she had a very feminine consciousness and a very masculine mind." Lubbock further observed that "it was once said of Edith Wharton, and she liked and repeated the remark, that she was a 'self-made man.' "[39]

A verbal slip that Wharton made in a letter to Bernard Berenson and herself caught and explained indicates that she thought of her creative self as masculine.[40] In speaking of Berenson's praise of her work, she says that it titillates "the author's vanity to have his pet phrases quoted to him," then adds in postscript, "You see I'm getting a little confused about my own sex!" (*Letters*, 398–99).

Wharton's being was further split between the retained and the rejected aspects of her mother. The negative side of her feminine heritage was boundaries, limitation, denial; its only positive signification was the option of becoming a "subject of adornment." She learned to value the ornamental side of femininity while repressing the sexual, not unlike her own Lily Bart of *The House of Mirth*. Edith always longed to emulate her mother's beauty and elegance, yet she was psychologically barred from becoming a mother or even fully a wife.

The fact that young Edith carried from her father's library into her mother's bedroom books from which she pretended to read what she had really invented indicates her desire to unite the sexual and the creative parts of herself, to bring her active self into the female realm and thereby to annihilate the artificial boundary between creation and her own feminine identity. Only at the end of her life, in her final novels, was Wharton able to imagine a way of doing this.

The loving and permissive father stands, in Wharton's memoirs, in marked contrast to the forbidding mother. There is a chiasmus here—a crossing-over of customary maternal and paternal traits that may be at the heart of Wharton's gender confusion. With her mother enthroned as the unsatisfiable super-ego and her father associated with the pleasures of indulgence, Wharton experienced a criss-crossing of identity lines. If we can follow them even a short way into the maze of gender identity, we may illuminate why Wharton invariably slipped into her female characterizations hints of masculinity. For example, the very "feminine" May Welland had large feet and hands too massive for needlework. She is described as athletic, boyish, and preferring strenuous hiking vacations to the cultural ones that Newland would have chosen. Female characters who write letters, such as Bertha Dorset of *The House of Mirth* and Elsie Ashby of the story "Pomegranate Seed," tend to have handwriting that incorporates "masculine curves" into a feminine script.

Wharton's fiction splits characters into polar opposites and splits situations into extreme alternatives. *The Old Maid* divides motherhood between a biological and a psychological mother. Fatherhood is radically split in *A Son at the Front*. Women characters are depicted in terms of polar oppositions in such stories as "The Touchstone."

Frequently, plot situations split into radical alternatives. The pregnant young Charity Royall (protagonist of *Summer*) had better options than marrying her adoptive father. She might have had an abortion or else gone to the city and found work to support her illegitimate child. The marriage effectually banished all of Charity's hopes for a fuller life. Chapter 4 will show that in *The Age of Innocence* Newland Archer himself forced the situation in which he had to sacrifice love for duty. This mildly artistic gentleman settles amiably for a limited destiny, not because, as so many believe, Wharton was ready to defend social conventions, but because Archer was too inhibited emotionally to seize what he thought he wanted. He could imagine more than he could grasp. Indeed, whenever a wayward impulse tempted him, he rushed into the protection of the nearest conventional obstacle. Surrounded by people who had learned to accommodate to change, to accept European manners and divorcées, he outdid his elders in conformity. His own exaggerated conventionalism created the prison house of rules that hemmed him in. In this he was very much like the young Edith Wharton who tortured herself with extreme and self-imposed moral scruples.

A reasonable middle way, though usually present and visible in Wharton's texts, seems psychically unattainable by characters who reflect the author's bias toward extreme alternatives. Thus the social constraints that lead to almost tragic destinies for Wharton's protagonists, that destroy Lily Bart and limit Newland Archer, are externalizations of psychic inhibitions, rationalizations for giving up the fullness of life. Wharton's narratives reflect the conflict between her powerful appetite for experience and the bonds she imposed on her own raging desires.

2

On the Threshold

To a torn heart uncomforted by human nearness a
room may open almost human arms, and the being to
whom no four walls mean more than any others, is, at
such hours, expatriate everywhere.

The House of Mirth

Despite a splendid income and a series of grand and beauti-
fully decorated houses, Edith Wharton felt herself insecurely
anchored in the world. The poignant words above convey her
irremediable sense of expatriation—her longing for a home
that would be an extension of parental protection, a shelter
for the vulnerable self. Ceaselessly, she sought the place that
would feel to her like a true home. First in America and then
in France she decorated houses with great zest and then rest-
lessly moved on to others. In her late fifties, after years of
exhausting work on behalf of people dispossessed by war,[1] she
would acquire two final estates that she inhabited alternately
according to the season. These country houses, one in the
suburbs of Paris, the other at Hyéres in southern France, allowed her to renew her passion for gardening.

The purchase of Ste. Claire, a winter home in the temperate
Riviera climate of Hyéres, was a satisfying move, one that she
experienced as coming home for the first time. She analogized
the acquisition of a home to marriage: "I feel as if I were going
to get married—to the right man at last!"[2] Her pleasure in
Ste. Claire was modified, however, by her inability to share a

home with anyone other than servants or to fill it with a family.

In *The House of Mirth*, published in 1905, Wharton isolates and intensifies her own variety of alienation. Here she magnifies her sense of maternal deprivation into Lily Bart's orphanhood. Lily's inner reality, like Wharton's, consists of ravenous hungers—insatiable needs for physical comfort, for security, for approbation. Lily also exhibits a variant of Wharton's own sexual inhibition and confusion, both particularly acute during the writing of this book. In Lily, Edith Wharton confronted the immature, narcissistic part of herself, but cast it into the body of the beautiful woman she longed to be. This chapter investigates what part of Wharton's sensibility was the "internal arena" that produced the doomed Lily Bart.[3]

SEXUAL SABOTAGE: *THE HOUSE OF MIRTH*

The title of *The House of Mirth* points toward its metaphorical nexus. Words representative of home—walls, shelter, refuge, nest—are linked here to the concept of love. The novel depicts the homeless heart and rootless existence of Lily Bart, a dazzlingly beautiful woman who cannot find a place for herself in the world. Lacking maternal sponsorship and financial resources, Lily desperately and ineffectually seeks marriage as a refuge for her frail selfhood.

The union of heart and home is the goal of most fictional marriage plots, in which a heroine meets both needs by finding a husband. For Lily Bart, as for Gwendolyn Harleth in George Eliot's *Daniel Deronda*, this classic expectation of novel readers is firmly denied. Both women love men who mirror their ideal selves (Selden and Deronda) but look to other men whom they do not love to provide the material foundation of their lives. Although Gwendolyn makes the kind of grand marriage that Lily seeks, this loveless choice proves a bitter disappointment and does not, in the long run provide either luxury or social position. Indeed, the two novels share

so many similarities in character and situation that their differences highlight Wharton's radical loneliness. Eliot's glitter-
ing heroine ends up drab and solitary, but she lives and
learns, and Daniel Deronda, her ideal love, marries in a way
that connects his future to his past. Even though Gwendolyn's
project fails, Deronda's marriage and hopeful prospects conclude the novel with affirmation. Wharton's heroine, on the
other hand, attains a momentary vision of the continuity of
human life, but dies, leaving the arc of her own life abruptly
truncated, and Lawrence Selden remains what he always
was, a bachelor-observer.[4]

Although language in *The House of Mirth* inextricably links
heart and home, the plot cannot bring the two together. For
example, Lily knows that "Selden's love could not be her ultimate refuge; only it would be so sweet to take a moment's
shelter there" (280). Gerty Farish imagines herself "at home"
in Lawrence Selden's heart, but cannot secure it for herself.
Only Nettie Struther, a poor working girl who had been in
trouble, was empowered by love "to gather up the fragments
of her life, and build herself a shelter with them" (517). A
major split in *The House of Mirth* comes from the fact that
Lily expects a husband to provide the sheltering walls, but
not intimacy. Such intimacy as she finds is entirely mental
and with a confirmed bachelor. When she seeks physical comfort, it is from motherly working-class women. In the soul of
Lily Bart, and very probably in that of her creator, heart and
home are tragically sundered.

Existentially as well as factually, Lily Bart is an orphan.
Both of her parents die before she is twenty-one, leaving her
impoverished and under the reluctant protection of an aunt
with whom she is temperamentally incompatible. She has to
struggle to keep afloat in a treacherous, competitive social
milieu without financial ballast or effective guidance into the
harbor of matrimony. Observing that a devoted and vigilant
mother was able to arrange prosperous marriages for the dull,
homely Van Osburgh girls, Lily concludes that the proper

social placement of a young woman can be accomplished only by a dedicated mother:

> Ah, lucky girls who grow up in the shelter of a mother's love, a mother who knows how to contrive opportunities without conceding favours. . . . The cleverest girl may miscalculate where her own interests are concerned, may yield too much at one moment and withdraw too far at the next; it takes a mother's unerring vigilance and foresight to land her daughters safely in the arms of wealth and suitability. (146)

Never having been "sheltered" in a mother's love, the beautiful Lily will never be sheltered in that of a husband.

Even before she lost her parents, Lily's family life had been unstable. "Ruling the turbulent element called home was the vigorous and determined figure of a mother still young enough to dance her ball-dresses to rags" and completely focused on her own social position. Their chaotic home was managed by an ever-changing series of nurses, maids, and footmen, "while the hazy outline of a neutral-tinted father filled an intermediate space between the butler and the man who came to wind the clocks" (45). This "effaced and silent" father is generally absent, either working late or left behind during the mother's frequent travels to fashionable watering places or on precipitate dashes to Paris to order trunks full of gowns.

Mr. Bart is of interest to his wife only so long as he is a provider. He exists to ensure that she has magnificent clothes and can afford to move in the right social circles. Otherwise she would be like ordinary people who, she says, "live like pigs." After Mr. Bart's financial ruin, she coldly awaits his death. "To his wife he no longer counted: he had become extinct when he ceased to fulfill his purpose; and she sat at his side with the provisional air of a traveler who waits for a belated train to start" (51). With the provider gone, Mrs. Bart expects Lily to repair her fortunes and relies on her daughter's beauty as if it were so much cash in the bank.

Lily's persistent confusion of sex with money is deeply rooted in her vision of family affairs. Just as Lily had seen her father exploited by her mother, she later saw Gus Trenor and George Dorset exploited by their wives, and she fully expects to exploit her husband when she lands one. Treated as a commodity herself, she rarely questions her intention to use others in the same way if necessary.[5]

Lily is so calculating about the marriage market that she is just as ready to use men as financial objects as they are to use her as a sexual object. About her value as an item of exchange she has learned to be remarkably clearheaded, thinking very much like a merchant needing to unload at the best possible price a self-destructing artifact. In view of this, her vagueness about real money is surprising. Not only does she spend her little income frivolously, she tries to recoup her follies by gambling at cards and loses even more. Too "feminine" to inquire just how Gus Trenor parlayed her small investment into a large sum, she never asks about how or when he ought to be reimbursed. She may think in market metaphors but knows nothing about money as an economic reality. It is just the magic something she needs to keep her luxuries flowing. And it comes from men.

The Bart family style and values caricature those of the Jones family—a stylish, socially obsessed mother with never quite enough money for her extravagant tastes, and a dim, compliant father who has a shy fondness for poetry. Clearly, Wharton is depicting her own family constellation, but with a crucial difference. Her memoir, we recall, opens with the dressed-up little Edith strolling with her handsome, loving father. His image dominates her picture of early family life, whereas at that stage her mother seemed dim and vague. Wharton regarded her father's admiration as the foundation of her feminine self, the origin of her pride in self-adornment.

Reliable love from her father and nanny had saved young Edith from complete depersonalization, whereas Lily Bart had insufficient contact with her father and had experienced a changing series of nursemaids. In a reversal of Wharton's family imagery, Lily's *mother* dominates the scene, leaving her father as only a vague absence. Because he worked such long hours that she rarely saw him, he could not provide for Lily the attention that might have compensated for maternal neglect. Wharton sets the decline of the Bart family's fortunes when Lily was nineteen, the author's age when her father's health failed.

Lacking a constant figure to whom she could attach herself, Lily fails to develop a viable core to her personality. Incessantly she seeks out mirrors to check on the continuity of her existence. Wharton's extreme closeness to her father may have retarded her sexual development, but Lily's deprivation of paternal contact seems to have left her incapable of attaining sexual maturity.

What raises Lily above her grasping mother is that her father's fondness for poetry inspires an artistic purpose that dilutes the family's crass mercantile objectives. Although Lily adopts her mother's values, she elevates them with a saving poetic sensibility, so that wealth becomes a means to enjoyment of beauty rather than mere materialism. She had "a vein of sentiment, perhaps transmitted from this source, which gave an idealizing touch to her most prosaic purposes. . . . She would not have cared to marry a man who was merely rich; she was secretly ashamed of her mother's crude passion for money" (54–55).

Lily's father-derived artistry is never developed by education or training. She can envision no material external to herself on which to exercise her innate artistry. With her own time-bound flesh as her only medium of expression, her matrimonial project requires youth and beauty. At the opening of *The House of Mirth*, Lily is almost thirty years old, has been too long on the marriage market, and has insufficient income to keep up her wardrobe. She recognizes that the commodity that she has become even to herself could grow stale on the shelf. She would then be unable to attract the wealthy husband whose function would be to sustain her self-image.[6]

Unable to visualize herself in any way of life less elegant

than high society (a social decline would mean, by her mother's values, living "like a pig"), she assumes that she must marry for wealth even if that means taking a dull husband. She has dichotomized her alternatives—she must be a permanently pampered beauty or else decline into piggery. The first is impossible, the second unthinkable.

Lily cannot mediate between the radical alternatives through which she perceives reality; she is unable to compromise or adapt. Incapable of imagining a middle state, such as living on a moderate income with a loving husband, Lily must achieve riches or die. We soon perceive that she herself unconsciously blocks off the avenues to riches, and after sliding rapidly down the social scale, she *does* die, presumably through suicide.

Lily is intrinsically and essentially a displaced person, one unfitted for the actualities of life. Homeless and rootless, she yearns to build around herself an environment that will protect and reflect her selfhood. Nothing in her aunt's tastelessly furnished home responds to her sensibilities or is really hers. She is "expatriate everywhere," a temporary sojourner in the homes of others. Jokingly but meaningfully, she tells Selden that she must marry in order to have a parlor of her own to furnish. For Lily, home is an extreme version of what it is for most women, an externalization of the self, a validation of the substantiality as well as the personality of that self. But Lily seems psychologically barred from attaining a durable home.

Whenever marital opportunity knocks, Lily turns inattentive. Ten years prior to the opening of the story, an Italian prince had wanted to marry her, but, as her match-making friend Carry Fisher shrewdly observes, "just at the critical moment a good-looking step-son turned up, and Lily was silly enough to flirt with him while her marriage-settlements were being drawn up. . . . That's Lily all over, you know; she works like a slave preparing the ground and sowing her seed; but the day she ought to be reaping the harvest she oversleeps herself or goes off on a picnic" (302–3). This telling vignette diagnoses the pattern of Lily's sexual behavior—flirtation with

the wrong man, often selected unconsciously to stir up oedipal rivalry, under the wrong circumstances, resulting in the
loss of genuine marital opportunities.

Even as she approaches the critical age of thirty, Lily continues to sabotage her marriage possibilities. She has kept her
sexuality split off from her marital ambitions and misdi-
rected her marital project into destructive flirtations with
unobtainable men—confirmed bachelors or the husbands of
her friends. By some fatality, Lily habitually situates herself
within dangerous oedipal triangles. Every such error reduces
her marriageability by generating gossip about her morals
and alienating her women friends. When she has virtually
secured a proposal from the wealthy Percy Gryce, she loses it
by violating his conventional pieties through smoking, gambling, and missing church services. Because Lawrence Selden, the man she loves, has only a modest income, she refuses
even to consider marrying him.

The scarcely interrogated barrier between Lily and Selden
is a curious donnée of the novel. Lily cannot think of compromising her demand for wealth or even enter into her calculus
the fact that as her Aunt Peniston's designated heir, she *can*
afford to marry Selden. Indeed, marriage to a respectable
gentleman like Selden would have served to secure Lily's inheritance. She loses it because of her own careless indiscre-
tions, by gambling and by allowing herself to become the
object of gossip.

We are left with the implication that this marriage, like all
others, is barred to Lily not by malignant social conditions
but by unconscious forces carried over from her creator. The
lady is not for marrying, but the novel refuses to examine this
premise, or even to state it. Lily is stuck on the verge of sexual
adulthood, unable to cross this threshold or to remain any
longer on it.

Whereas Wharton protects Lily's sexual inhibitions from
ready detection by camouflaging them with financial motives, she enjoys exposing Selden's resistance to marriage by
means of continuous innuendo. He seems almost asexual, de-

spite the plot mechanism of his prior love affair with Bertha
Dorset. A resident of an apartment house called The Benedick
and always relieved when his approaches to Lily are rebuffed
with the "insufficient funds" argument, he seems to be one of
the confirmed bachelors that Wharton first came to know in
the person of Walter Berry.

Lily approaches the marital project in ignorance of its personal and sexual dimension. With flirtation and wedlock split
off from sexuality, she understands marriage only in terms of
property, never of desire. She dismisses too easily the prompt-
ings of desire that she feels for Selden because they fail to
connect to property and hence to security. When she decides
that she must accept Rosedale,

> she did not indeed let her imagination range beyond the day of
> plighting; after that everything faded into a haze of material
> well-being, in which the personality of her benefactor re-
> mained mercifully vague. She had learned . . . that there were
> certain things not good to think of, certain midnight images
> that must at any cost be exorcised—and one of these was the
> image of herself as Rosedale's wife. (400)

Lily's expressed misgivings about Rosedale's "race" may obscure the implication of these exorcised midnight images,
surely visions of the marriage bed, which seem to be carried
over from Wharton's own nightmares.

Almost inevitably, Lily is perceived as the obverse of
Undine Spragg, the equally beautiful heroine of *The Custom of
the Country* (1913). Whereas Lily, the perfect lady, sabotages
all attempts to achieve her goals, the emotionally and verbally crude Undine attains success at every endeavor, marrying first into New York society and then into French nobility.
Whereas Lily never achieves marriage, Undine Spragg Moffatt Marvell de Chelles Moffatt (to list all the surnames she
acquires in the course of the book) does so repeatedly. Undine
captures every husband she targets as well as every luxury,
yet is perpetually dissatisfied.

Both women share the motto "Beyond!", which is the word

inscribed on Lily's seal. Undine recognizes that she is driven to seek always for the desire that is *beyond* her present attainment: "There was something still better beyond, then—more luxurious, more exciting, more worthy of her . . . it was always her fate to find out just too late about the something beyond" (54).

This longing for the unattained is probably the mark of the artist in both of them, but in Undine it represents, as Cynthia Griffin Wolff emphasizes, the state of being driven by unfocused, infantile desire. To desire "everything," as Undine does, is to desire nothing in particular. Drive without an object is probably the supreme form of restlessness, and, as Wolff clearly recognizes, Wharton endowed Undine with her own unmanageable energy.[7]

One heroine is passive, the other relentlessly driven, one slides downhill, whereas the other climbs, but both lack the capacity for sexual intimacy. Although *The Custom of the Country* is a novel of the imperious self demanding its rights, fulfillment of sexual desire is not among these demands.[8] In marriage, Undine "regarded intimacy as a pretext for escaping from [social] forms into a total absence of expression" (151). Her sexual response was "remote and Ariel-like, suggesting from the first, not so much of the recoil of ignorance as the coolness of the element from which she took her name" (152).

Lily Bart's innocence in flirting with the husbands of her friends comes from a radical ignorance of the connections between biology and social institutions. She suffers from an acquired ignorance similar to the kind that caused Edith Wharton to enter marriage unprepared. Denying the fact of male as well as female desire, Lily misjudges the consequences of displaying her thinly clad body at the *tableau vivante* and assumes that the event had been all triumph. When she complies with her friends' requests to divert the attention of their husbands, she fails to recognize the dangers of the game as well as the provocative signals that she has been sending to the husbands.

Lily misreads social cues such as Gus Trenor's sincere belief that he has earned her sexual favors. The exhibition of her body at the *tableau* leads Gus to think that if she is thus accessible to every man, he, who has lent her money, should be the first to collect. When he tries to trap her into paying up, Lily is forced to confront raw sexual reality. She tries to deny this by disingenuously interpreting Gus's demand as a request for repayment of money, and when she realizes that Gus considers her favors already bought and paid for, she is horrified.

This is a pivotal moment in the novel. Lily has had an artistic triumph in the *tableau*, but her friends are beginning to mock her. After gossip columnists make sly insinuations about the way she has exposed herself, cousin Jack dissociates himself by pretending shock at "a girl standing up there as if she was up at auction." He thinks she had better marry quickly, even to so unlikely a partner as the Jew Rosedale, because "in Lily's circumstances it's a mistake to have too high a standard" (254–55).

Feeling that Lily's behavior has been misunderstood, Selden is moved to rescue her by marriage. At this point she could either lose her marginal place in the world or gain a firm one. She can still make or mar her fortunes, but she cannot continue in the same track. At this juncture, her sudden confrontation with Gus Trenor's raw sexuality determines Lily's downward course. Because Lawrence Selden happens accidentally to witness her departure from Gus's house when he knows that Gus's wife is away, he concludes that Lily is incorrigibly careless of her reputation. In disgust he leaves town without proposing marriage or explaining his sudden departure. What appears to be unfortunate coincidence or just another instance of Lily's bad luck is actually an irony critical to the underlying structure of this novel: *without having committed or desired adultery, Lily must pay the price of it.*

The failed seduction scene is, as critic Joan Lidoff noted, "written entirely in the rising and completed rhythms of sexual climax."[9] To Gus's touch and his "puffing face" Lily reacts with accelerated pulses, limpness, and other physiological reactions common to sexual arousal, but experienced by Lily as terror. The focus of her terror is Gus's hand, which "grew formidable" as he drew closer (235). (Her reaction to this swelling appendage accords with considerable other textual evidence that Wharton regarded the hand as something of a sexual organ.) Lily's terror and contempt deflate Gus's ardor, allowing her to flee his house physically intact, but in emotional chaos.

She is devastated not by anger at her close encounter with rape, but by shame and guilt. She feels defiled by a catastrophic revelation, hunted by the Furies, "alone in a place of darkness and pollution" (239). Turning up distraught at the home of Gerty Farish, Lily declares that she is "bad—a bad girl—all my thoughts are bad. . . . There are bad girls in your slums. Tell me—do they ever pick themselves up? Ever forget, and feel as they did before?" (266). She now feels less honorable than these whores: "I've sunk lower than the lowest, for I've taken what they take and not paid as they pay" (268–69).

Why does she feel shame instead of anger, and why such extreme self-degradation? Why should Gus Trenor's readily foiled sexual approaches make this inviolable woman feel defiled? Why does she transfer to herself, the victim of a crude attempt at seduction, so much shame that her final act in life is to send her desperately needed inheritance check to Gus, who never sought return of the money? The nature of Lily's response and its extremity break through the social envelope of the novel, taking us back to the arena of the author's sexual confusion, straight to young Edith's tendency to feel polluted by even her unuttered thoughts, her need to atone for any thoughts that were "not nice," that is, sexual.

Lily Bart, by playing up to her close friends' husbands in the hope of being cared for financially, has been playing with oedipal fire. The very women who encourage her to do this in order to distract their husbands' attention from their own flirtations turn against her as if she had been seeking to displace them. Without even desiring her friends' husbands, she is treated as a sexual rival and suffers consequences appropriate to such a role. Indeed, in blaming herself for Gus's seduction attempt, Lily Bart acts and feels very much like many victims of incest, who tend to assume moral responsibility for their own abuse. Rather than blame their fathers or brothers, they assume that their own guilty thoughts provoke the assaults, and they react with self-loathing.[10]

Following the sexual threat, Lily's view of herself and the world is radically altered. She feels herself pursued by Furies, with nowhere to hide. Feeling polluted by her first exposure to frank sexuality, she is unable to return to the immaculate home of her aunt. In her own social world, "drawing rooms are always tidy" and unmarried girls always chaste; to find acceptance she must drop into the world of the working class.

Despite the late hour she feels driven to the only door where she can find rest and comfort. And that door belongs to Gerty Farish, Lawrence Selden's drab cousin—a simple, loving woman who works for a living. Constructed as a negation of Lily's narcissism, this social worker seems to have no self of her own. To all appearances, she lives only for others, and most especially for her idealized Lily, whom she yearns to protect.

These two young women in polar opposition (both in love with Selden) have special meaning for each other and for the structure of the novel. They represent a division of femininity into drab usefulness and useless ornamentation, neither of these extremes being efficacious in the biological world of sexual competition. Within the novel, neither will be selected to mate. Representing Lily's feared negative identity of a drab, constricted life, Gerty can offer comfort in a crisis but not a model of capable womanhood. She is without power in Lily's social world, very much like a nanny.

And it is as a nanny-equivalent that Gerty functions in *The House of Mirth*. It is to Gerty that Lily flees when terrified by irrational fears. She knows that regardless of Gerty's own needs the door will open to her even in the middle of the night. On this particular night, Lily's midnight visit is not really welcome because Gerty has just begun to thrill to the hope that Lawrence Selden may possibly love her. Usually selfless, Gerty has developed hopes of a life of her own, rather than one of service to others. Just as she is awakening to the claims of her own desires, she is forced to recognize that Selden prefers Lily. For a brief moment, she hates Lily for being her rival. But as a social worker and professional caretaker, Gerty has learned to discipline her emotions. She puts them aside and calmly cares for the distraught woman who needs her.

Lily needs to be held together physically and emotionally. She craves "the darkness made by enfolding arms, the silence that is not solitude, but compassion holding its breath" (240). She wants to be warmed by Gerty, held by Gerty, even to sleep in Gerty's narrow bed.

> "Hold me, Gerty, hold me, or I shall think of things," she moaned; and Gerty silently slipped an arm under her, pillowing her head into its hollow as a mother makes a nest for a tossing child. In the warm hollow Lily lay still and her breathing grew low and regular. Her hand still clung to Gerty's as if to ward off evil dreams, but the hold of her fingers relaxed, her head sank deeper into its shelter, and Gerty felt that she slept. (270)

Gerty's body becomes a nest, a shelter, a home for this fitful, childlike woman. Lily relies on Gerty like a child on its nanny, oblivious to the possibility that Nanny may have concerns or interests of her own. The child has needs and the professional nurturer fills them.

In the course of the novel Lily passes through a steadily declining series of maternal surrogates until she reaches the bottom of the social ladder. After her worldly, trivial mother and a sanctimonious, wealthy aunt, and socialite friends Judy Trenor and Bertha Dorset, she slips down to lower levels of the nouveau riche. With these false mothers she is usually trapped into costly entanglements with the husbands, leading to banishment from their homes. With each banishment she has to step down to meaner and drabber living quarters. After losing her wealthy protectors she tries, with little success, to work for a living. At the end of the series, in a kind of fortunate fall, she basks in the kindly warmth of Nettie Struther, a working-class woman.

There are good mother-figures in *The House of Mirth*, and though insufficient for Lily's needs they try to move her toward the resolution of her severe identity problems. Gerty Farish offers succor and protection that for snobbish reasons Lily cannot completely accept. Carry Fisher, a divorcée operating on the margins of good society, behaves with almost disinterested maternal concern in sharing opportunities with Lily and trying to arrange a realistic marriage for her. Each fulfills some aspect of a mother's role, but they do not suffice.

All the mother-figures are way stations in Lily's slide to her final encounter at the bottom of the social ladder. Here, totally exhausted and destitute, she finds Nettie Struther, a former recipient of public charity, now married and mother of an infant daughter. Nettie's life has been moving in the opposite direction from Lily's—upward from despair.

Nettie's experience with sex had been genuinely distressing; it resulted in an out-of-wedlock pregnancy. But instead of writing herself off as a polluted woman, she made pragmatic choices and reconstructed her life. She has married a man who can accept her child, and she is building a home for herself and her baby. This home is humble but sufficient to shelter life and sustain continuity: "It had the frail, audacious permanence of a bird's nest built on the edge of a cliff—a mere wisp of leaves and straw, yet so put together that the lives entrusted to it may hang safely over the abyss" (517). For Nettie, home and heart unite to form a structure that, however fragile, can be trusted.

Although sophisticated critics may view the poor but courageous Nettie Struther and her baby as refugees from a sentimental novel, the pair are tied into the deeper themes of *The House of Mirth*. Nettie's frail shelter is built from womanly courage, adaptability, and the capacity for love. Her self-image allows for accommodation and regeneration, capacities that the beautiful Lily Bart lacks. Whereas Nettie could make a home for her illegitimate child, Lily becomes emotionally fragmented by an easily foiled attempt at seduction. Wharton may have cast into Lily Bart the sexual fears of her young womanhood, but at this time in her life she could imagine other options for women. Lily is out of touch with her desires, but Nettie and the adulterous Bertha Dorset are not.

The exchange of benefits between Nettie and Lily reflects the difference between narcissism and altruism. Lily, to make herself feel good, had visited a women's club and donated some spare cash to send Nettie to a tuberculosis sanitarium. Having been motivated more by vanity than charity, Lily scarcely even remembers the recipient of her benefactions. But Nettie has used the idealized memory of Lily's help to enhance her own self-worth. She has used it to re-attach herself to life, and she seeks an opportunity to pass back the gift to her former benefactress.

She babies Lily, taking her into the warm kitchen and feeding her. Considering the social difference, one might have expected Nettie to bring her elegant guest into the parlor. But parlors symbolize the social world that has failed Lily. In Nettie's shabby but warm working-class kitchen, Lily can experience the "continuity of life" just before her own extinction.

Into Lily's arms Nettie places her baby, whom she had named "Marry-Anto'nette" after the role played by an actress who reminded her of Lily. The baby's name and its acceptance of her nurturance gently bring Lily into the chain of human generation. Holding this new life somehow named in her honor clarifies for her the great arc of her existence, the relationship of her past to her present and of both past and present to her future prospects. She has for the first time a "vision of the solidarity of life" (516).

But the facts of Lily's existence cannot sustain this sense of beatitude. Back in her solitary room she feels the "reaction of a deeper loneliness" (511).

> It was no longer, however, from the vision of material poverty that she turned with the greatest shrinking. She had a sense of deeper empoverishment—of an inner destitution compared to which outward conditions dwindled into insignificance. . . . It

was the clutch of solitude at her heart . . . the feeling of being
something rootless and ephemeral, mere spin-drift of the whirl-
ing surface of existence, without anything to which the poor
little tentacles of self could cling before the awful flood sub-
merged them. And as she looked back she saw that there had
never been a time when she had any real relation to life. Her
parents too had been rootless . . . without any personal existence to shelter them from its shifting gusts. She herself had
grown up without any one spot of earth being dearer to her
than another. . . . [She had no connection] to all the mighty
sum of human striving. (515–16)

In her drab boardinghouse room she reviews her lovely
gowns, relics of past triumphs, settles her accounts, and generally puts her affairs in order. After taking a sleeping draught
she falls into a sensuous slumber, imagining that Nettie's
baby is lying on her arm.

Suddenly she understood why she did not feel herself alone. . . .
She felt the pressure of its little head against her shoulder. She
did not know how it had come there, but she felt no great
surprise at the fact, only a gentle penetrating thrill of warmth
and pleasure. She settled herself into an easier position, hollow-
ing her arm to pillow the round, downy head and holding her
breath lest a sound should disturb the sleeping child. (517)

Lily offers the baby precisely what she herself had received
from Gerty Farish when shivering with terror in the middle of
the night—warmth and gentle, empathic holding. The two
parallel episodes are described in almost the same words.
Having found her way back to the peace and satisfaction of
infancy through identification with the infant that she herself
has nurtured, Lily is ready to return to death, the great
mother.

Gerty's kindness following Lily's sexual fright anticipates
Nettie's nurturant acts.[11] Gerty had provided the kind of one-
way comfort of which Lily had been deprived in childhood. In
contrast, Nettie's kindness extends nurturance into a linked
chain of human care. Having formerly received benefits from
Lily, Nettie welcomes an opportunity to reciprocate. By in-

cluding Lily in the act of mothering an infant, Nettie enables her to reach beyond narcissism into imagining an "other" and nurturing it. Both Gerty and Nettie are working women, but with the difference that Gerty, as a well-connected social worker, bridges two social classes, whereas Nettie, fully of and from the working class, is able to place Lily in connection to "the mighty sum of human striving" (516).

A HOUSE OF MIRRORS

Although I have been arguing for psychological rather than social determinants in *The House of Mirth*, the book clearly has a social dimension. This lies in its challenge to the common assumptions that marriage is the only destiny for a woman and that adornment is her main function. Accepting these assumptions, Lily Bart measures herself by her ornamental value. For such a woman, identity derives from admiration reflected in the eyes of others. This is indeed a socially constructed female role, one particularly significant for Wharton because her mother had played it so well and because she herself still felt drawn to it. Had cultural constraints been the core of the novel, it might have had an ironic ending, as in *The Custom of the Country*. But as an example of a cultural phenomenon, Lily's case is exaggerated.

In the course of her downhill slide through society, Lily sees many ways in which women of her time functioned within their social system. Many of them structured their lives without making themselves into ornamental objects for sale on the marriage market. Gerty Farish is an unmarried, self-supporting social worker. Carry Fisher, a divorced mother, manages to make her own living as a social facilitator. Women own and manage shops, make hats, work in factories. Class assumptions about women's roles do limit Lily's thinking, but the presence of these alternatives in *The House of Mirth* weakens the commonly accepted idea that she was destroyed entirely by external forces.

Lily's definition of herself as one condemned to be "a moment's ornament" (the original title of the book) is intensified by narcissism stemming from maternal deprivation. She had grown up thinking she had to earn her place by pleasing others, and her beauty seemed the likeliest way to accomplish this. Wharton tossed us a red herring when she treated *The House of Mirth* as a realistic social novel. She asked rhetorically how "a society of irresponsible pleasure-seekers [could] be said to have . . . any deeper bearing than the people composing such a society could guess? The answer was that a frivolous society can acquire dramatic significance only through what its frivolity destroys. Its tragic implication lies in its power of debasing people and ideals. The answer, in short, was my heroine, Lily Bart" (*Backward Glance*, 207). Wharton's own statement that society destroyed Lily Bart helped establish Wharton as a social critic and novelist of manners, an impression reinforced by her distinct talent for social satire.

Accepting this view in *No Man's Land* (1989), Sandra Gilbert and Susan Gubar treat Lily's story as "determinedly and deterministically sociological," written by a "cultural determinist in the mode of Thorstein Veblen," who was bent on proving that women are forced into enslavement as either "prisoners of sex" or "sex parasites." Believing that Wharton's plots were driven by "an impassioned disgust with the laws governing the world that Veblen described," Gilbert and Gubar tend to regard the "individual adventures" of Wharton's heroines as representative of women of their time and class.[12]

Only rarely has this conception been challenged. In a pioneering article, Joan Lidoff wrote in 1980 that *The House of Mirth* "purports to be a novel of social realism" but is really a "romance of identity . . . controlled by a deeper dynamic."[13] She argued that Wharton's "confounding of realism with romance" led to a structural flaw in the novel.[14]

Wharton's capacity to criticize her inherited social world

may have been limited by the same paradoxical affection that she identified in Proust:

> His greatness lay in his art, his incredible littleness in the quality of his social admirations. But in this, after all, he merely exemplified the tendency not infrequent in novelists of manners—Balzac and Thackeray among them—to be dazzled by contact with the very society they satirize. If it is true that *pour comprendre il faut aimer* this seeming inconsistency may, in some, be a deep necessity of the creative imagination. (*Backward Glance*, 325)

Like Proust, Edith Wharton remained dazzled by the society whose limitations she was uniquely positioned to recognize.

Lily's defeat is not wholly the result of social determinants, nor is her death a capitulation to sentimental literary conventions. Both are direct results of her inability to move beyond narcissistic enjoyment of her own beauty into sharing it fully with another. She dies on the threshold of female sexuality, unable to cross over.

When Lily realizes at the end of chapter 3 that she cannot attain the independent life that other women have forged, she resigns herself to her narcissistic pursuit. "She knew that she hated dinginess as much as her mother had hated it, and to her last breath she meant to fight against it, dragging herself up again and again above its flood until she gained the bright pinnacles of success which presented such a slippery surface to her clutch" (61).

This passion for beauty helps explain why readers love and identify with such a narcissistic heroine as Lily Bart. Wharton manages to give Lily's yearning for admiration and luxury the status of a much nobler quest—the quest for secure possession of beauty. Sharing Wharton's love of beauty, but being herself a work of art rather than a creator of it, Lily is as ephemeral as mortal beauty, traditionally symbolized by a flower. The transience of beauty is part of her pathos. Her passion to sustain and perpetuate it enlarges her endeavors. The sympathy with which Wharton depicts Lily's yearning differentiates her from other narcissistic heroines of literature such as Becky Sharp and Scarlett O'Hara, but most particularly from Lily's own obverse image, Undine Spragg of *The Custom of the Country*.

To enhance her value on the marriage market, Lily makes herself into an exquisite visual object, the Perfect Lady always displayed to advantage. She displays her radiant beauty against dark backgrounds—trees and shadows as well as the drabness of the everyday world. We first see Lily through the eyes of Lawrence Selden, in the heat and tumult of Grand Central Station: "Selden had never seen her more radiant. Her vivid head, relieved against the dull tints of the crowd, made her more conspicuous than in a ball-room" (4).

The piquancy of transience also sets off Lily's radiance. Both Lily and Selden are aware that she is twenty-nine years old, almost thirty, when ladies are expected to have faded into matrons. Selden is just connoisseur enough to appreciate the moment of transition, to enjoy watching Lily's games on this temporal boundary. Wharton presents this encounter entirely in visual terms, with Selden as spectator and Lily as the object of his almost detached speculation.

It is a game they play together. Lily controls the angle and the lighting by which she will be seen. She knows how to adjust background and gestures to the tastes of her viewer—idealistic but seductive for Lawrence Selden, virginal and pious for Percy Gryce. She directs her most deceptive wiles toward Gryce, for whom she has little respect. She presents her finer self to the connoisseur Selden, who is her ideal audience, the one who misses few nuances of her behavior. He is the chosen witness of Lily's best self—of her moral as well as her aesthetic performances.

She is so pleasing an aesthetic object that she has learned to experience herself only insofar as she is reflected in the eyes of others. Lily relishes her own beauty by seeing it through Selden's eyes. She seems an extreme version of a trait that one theorist attributes to women in general, a tendency to be split between *being* a visual object and *seeing herself* as a visual object. Says John Berger: "The woman must continually watch herself . . . While she is walking across a room or whilst she is weeping at the death of her father, she can scarcely avoid envisaging herself walking or weeping. . . . The surveyor of woman in herself is male; the surveyed female."[15]

Always author, director, manager, and star of her own theatrical production, Lily also incorporates the audience, or viewer, so that she can imagine herself as perceived by the other. With the aid of this double perspective, Lily masters the art of dress and the languages of gesture, tone, light, and setting. This division of herself into subject and object enables her to manipulate the impression she makes on men. Although a degree of self-objectification is a normal part of the mating game, Lily's extreme investment in herself as object reduces her capacity for subjective wholeness.

Having lacked empathic mirroring in her childhood, Lily is always seeking and constructing her own reflection. She cannot resist her mirrored image, whether it be to admire it or to study it for signs of aging. She also seeks her reflection in the good and bad, flattering or warped, mirrors of other people's perceptions. Her identity diminishes to the insubstantiality of a reflected image.

She becomes very uneasy when left alone. On a solitary forest walk near Bellomont, Lily finds that "the sparkle had died out of her, and the taste of life was stale on her lips. . . . [She felt] an inner desolation deeper than the loneliness about her" (97). "She was not accustomed to the joys of solitude except in company" (97). When Lily shows signs of aging, and her reflected image declines in value, she loses her hold on life. So closely related to mirrors is Lily's existence that the mirror above her vanity table shows empty following her death. Selden, surveying her few last effects in her dingy boarding-house room, shrinks "from the blank surface of the toilet-mirror" (528).

In making a spectacle of herself—in making herself into an object of speculation—for all to interpret, Lily can awe and impress, but she cannot fully control audience response. She can manage her effects on certain receptive men, but not, alas, on other women. As she exits from her innocent but imprudent visit to Lawrence Selden's apartment, she comes under the merciless gaze of his charwoman. Lily tries with elegant hauteur to subdue the woman's bold appraisal. Unable to do this, she realizes that the stout, red-fisted charwoman's "persistent gaze implied a groping among past associations," that is, she is placing Lily among loose women who visit men's apartments. Lily's fine clothes and hauteur serve only to intensify the scrubwoman's speculations.

Virtually all circumstances in *The House of Mirth* conspire to focus sexual speculation about the person of Lily Bart, a woman who is unable to *face* her own sexuality, much less to act on it. Despite her skill at manipulating her image, she is almost invariably seen under compromising conditions that suggest that she is a "fast" woman if not a loose one. Her own unconscious or that of Edith Wharton inevitably places her in the spotlight of unacknowledged desire, causing her to lose control of the situations that matter most to her.

She cannot control the perceptions of Simon Rosedale, the one man who is her potential match. He sees her coming out of Lawrence Selden's apartment building and immediately sees through her fib about visiting her dressmaker. Rosedale turns up regularly, aware of Lily's every false move and indiscretion and deducting these from her current value on the marriage market.[16] Underestimating his shrewdness, she thinks of him as her last resource, someone she can marry if all else fails. But when, at the nadir of her fortunes, she tries to draw on this resource, she learns that Rosedale will marry her only on condition that she recover her value as a social asset. He demands that she use her possession of Bertha Dorset's love letters to Selden as a form of blackmail that will ensure their joint social dominance over Bertha. To her credit, Lily refuses to stoop to such means.[17]

Simon Rosedale is an almost omniscient observer. He alone of the important male spectators of Lily Bart's life reads her accurately. Percy Gryce was deceived for a while and might have remained so had Lily been able to control her behavior. Gus Trenor has the wrong script. And Lawrence Selden, relying on his habitual detachment, misreads her because he does not understand himself.

Wharton attributes paradoxical qualities to Rosedale, the Jewish man of business who is socially "impossible" in Lily's set. His very name, an anglicization of Rosenthal, suggests his determination to pass into a social world that would reject a Jew. The author's implication is ambivalent when she says that he has "his race's accuracy in the appraisal of values." Indeed, Rosedale combines the very qualities on which Wharton prided herself, "artistic sensibility and business astuteness" (23–24)—the ability to appreciate quality and the lucidity to appraise its proper value. Although not verbally sophisticated like Lawrence Selden, another connoisseur, Rosedale can recognize the best article on the market, calculate its value to himself at any given moment, control his sexual feelings when they interfere with his long-range goals, yet act to seize what he really wants. He is masterful in practical matters and a connoisseur in aesthetic ones.

Although hampered socially by what Wharton calls his "race," he is wealthy enough to pamper Lily's luxurious tastes and looks forward to doing so. He is genuinely kind, as we know from his gentleness with Carry Fisher's little girl when no one is present to observe it. Simon Rosedale understands himself. He can be generous to others but has no intention of undermining his social ambitions by acting with sentimental folly. In many ways, Rosedale is a man to reckon with, and one after Edith Wharton's heart.

That this despised Jew should be the man best fitted to provide for Lily because of his accurate and unsentimental appraisal of her is very much related to the strange sexual behavior of Lily Bart and the psychosexual development of her creator. Although the book may seem to be a failed *pas de deux* between Lily and Selden, her idealized love, the synchronized movements between Lily and Rosedale—the movements from attraction to aversion to affinity—shadow and finally control the stage-front actions. The fateful dance and the most significant one is the subtle ballet between the Lily and the Rose.

Rosedale is the spectre of the incestuous figure who haunts Wharton's imagination, the provider or father surrogate, sometimes labeled a Levantine, who both entices the heroine and appalls her.[18] We shall track a circuitous route before we see that this figure ultimately stands for Wharton's unresolved feelings about her father, neither Levantine nor Americanized Jew, but the tabooed "other" of Wharton's early years.

3

The Passion Experience

I felt for the first time that indescribable current of
communication flowing between myself & some one
else—felt it, I mean uninterruptedly, securely, so that
it penetrated every sense & every thought . . . & said
to myself: "This must be what happy women feel."

I have drunk of the wine of life at last, I have known
the thing best worth knowing, I have been warmed
through and through, never to grow quite cold again
till the end.

"The Love Diary"

Wharton recognized that to liberate her sexual nature, she
must wrestle with her internalized mother and force from it
the nurturance she needed. To illustrate this process, we focus
on a major event, her love affair with Morton Fullerton, and
examine two fictional creations that bracket it—first and prin-
cipally, "The Touchstone," a novella written years before she
met him but oddly predictive of aspects of the relationship,
and second, *The Reef,* a novel written a few years after passion
had departed. Edith Wharton used both stories to work on
and if possible to work out life problems troubling her at the
respective times. Written a dozen years apart, these two
works stand here as examples of prediction and postdiction
about a central event in Wharton's life, her first experience of
passionate love.

REWORKING THE MATERNAL IMAGERY:
"THE TOUCHSTONE"

In "The Touchstone" (written and published in 1900, her thirty-eighth year) she tried to devise a way in which a separation of the good mother from the bad one might be accomplished. She set into dramatic interaction fragments of herself and of key childhood figures, but rather than have them reenact past scenes, she let them play out a reparative script that would refashion the maternal imagery.[1] "The Touchstone" is a story of guilt, of spiritual redemption, of attaining adulthood by working through unfinished maternal relationships. It enacts a process of spiritual rebirth that the author longed to achieve for herself.

The plot of "The Touchstone" manipulates various levels of Wharton's formative experiences as they impinged on her current problems. The narrative course is set by her guilt for negative feelings toward her mother and a deep need to renegotiate the relationship before it was too late. In 1900 her mother was paralyzed and near death in distant Paris. Although living in various places on the east coast during this time, Wharton was making frequent trips to Europe, including Paris, but rarely visited her. Wharton's very efforts to rid herself of the reproving maternal image served only to increase her guilt. Her mother's impending death, which occurred in 1901, would forever bar her from repairing the actual relationship. At this critical time Wharton was fighting her way out of a long period of depression and beginning to perceive herself as a professional writer. Each act that marked a separation of past and future, such as abandoning her place in Newport society and building her own home in Lenox, Massachusetts, each expression of her long-denied autonomy generated guilt as well as exhilaration.

Wharton came to realize that her now-remote actual mother was less important to her than the internalized one that was inhibiting her autonomy. If the omnipresent accusing mother was part of herself and to some degree her own creation, it might be susceptible to modification. Her way of working on this was to incorporate into the character of the novelist Margaret Aubyn not only troubling aspects of herself as woman and writer, but also aspects of the mother she carried within, the creation of her own childish psyche that she now needed to exorcise or transform. Removing the mother-daughter antagonism from the actual interpersonal arena and locating it within the daughter's psyche renders the struggle independent of time, space, and the real mother's actions or intentions.

Writing "The Touchstone" facilitated Wharton's transition into personal and professional autonomy. It reads like a projective vision of events waiting to happen, a life script to be enacted as soon as Wharton found the right actor for the male lead. In devising this story of a woman's one-sided, selfless love for an immature man, Wharton formed a template by which she would recognize the kind of emotional experience she was seeking unconsciously. Indeed, reading "The Touchstone" prospectively in the light of the later Fullerton affair helps us understand Wharton's puzzling relationship with this man.

The tale depicts the spiritual-emotional growth of an impoverished young lawyer, Stephen Glennard, who, needing money to marry a beautiful and equally impoverished young woman, surreptitiously sells love letters written to him by Margaret Aubyn, a deceased novelist who had once loved him. Only after Margaret's death does he realize to what extent she had infiltrated his soul. The marriage he achieves with the proceeds from sale of her letters is damaged by his feelings of guilt for having betrayed Aubyn's selfless love for him. The spirit of the dead novelist seems to him like that of an accusing mother whom he has wronged. His project, then, is to transmute this persecutory mother-figure into an enabling one.

The author cast certain aspects of herself as the ardent but graceless novelist Margaret Aubyn and other aspects of herself as Stephen Glennard, a man oppressed by the memory of

Aubyn's generosity. In the multivalent character of Margaret Aubyn, Wharton reworked specific elements that derived from her own past, reflected her present, and anticipated her future. As an unappeasable conscience figure, Aubyn represents the persecutory aspect of Wharton's inner mother, and as a formidable woman writer with little confidence in her sexual desirability, she represents aspects of Wharton herself at the time of writing. Given Aubyn's multiple functions in the story, she represents not the self-centered, withholding aspects of Wharton's actual mother, but rather the obverse, a masochistic mother figure who achieves psychic omnipresence by inducing guilt. Furthermore, as a character who found fulfillment by giving feminine nurturance and forgiveness to an ungrateful man, she became a prophetic model for Wharton's future relationship with Morton Fullerton.

Wharton depicted Margaret Aubyn much as she imagined she herself might be perceived by men—as a homely and aggressively intellectual woman. Wharton feared that no matter how smartly she might dress, men would miss her essential femininity. She felt particularly self-conscious about the jutting lower jaw that marred the shape of her lower lip, a characteristic that Kenneth Clark, a devoted friend, called "her letter-box mouth, always her least attractive feature."[2] Of the consequences of such a defect, she wrote: "Just such a hair-breadth deflection from the line of beauty as had determined the curve of Mrs. Aubyn's lips" (11) made her "incapable . . . of any hold upon the pulses" (4). Aubyn's moral superiority and "intellectual ascendancy" had made Glennard feel his own inferiority (11). She "combined with a kind of personal shyness an intellectual audacity that was like a deflected impulse of coquetry: one felt that if she had been prettier she would have had emotions instead of ideas" (10).

In short, says the narrator, "the attitude of looking up is a strain on the muscles; and it was becoming more and more Glennard's opinion that brains, in a woman, should be merely the obverse of beauty" (11–12). Although Edith Wharton was not yet a celebrated writer in 1900, we can easily see that whomever else Margaret Aubyn may have resembled,[3] her creator was describing her own insecurities as a woman while imagining how achieving authorial success would serve only to exacerbate them. She was using "The Touchstone" to help locate and define a style of femininity compatible with childlessness and professional ambition, a style in which she herself could be successful.

To Stephen Glennard, Wharton consigned that part of herself seeking redemption from maternal tyranny. To him she entrusted the task of discovering the hidden beneficence, the occult capacity for nurturance folded into his inner vision of the dead Margaret Aubyn. Release of this hidden power required a violent personal agon. With the help of a spiritual guide in the form of his wife Alexa, Glennard is able to modify the destructive maternal image, to revise or rewrite it.

The story leads him through despair and guilt to a rebirth into fuller and freer adulthood. His violation of Aubyn's trust by publishing her letters and using the proceeds to fund his marriage to a second woman had generated a disabling sense of guilt. This moral lapse functions in the story as a "fall" that finally he must convert into something positive, an opportunity for emotional growth. By the end, he finds a way to liberate himself from the oppressive mother-figure that he had internalized as a voice of perpetual accusation. Having mastered the emotional alchemy necessary to transmute the negative presence into a nurturing one, he is freed to take on an adult role within his marriage.

Because the Aubyn-Glennard relationship occurred prior to the opening of the novella, it functions as a "prehistoric" event that haunts Glennard's life and diminishes his capacity for adult love. Glennard's revulsion against physical contact with such a mother figure as Aubyn serves a dual purpose in the story. Beyond signifying an oedipal barrier, it blinds him to Aubyn's essential femininity. Until he adjusts his relationship to this "first" woman, he can merely play-act the role of husband to the second. His marriage starts as a shallow pretense, symbolized by a picture-book house that "seemed no more than a gay tent pitched against the sunshine" (28). For it to become a sturdy home that could withstand storms, Glennard must free himself from his mother-surrogate. First he must confront his disabling sense of guilt.

He finds himself imprisoned in "the windowless cell of . . . consciousness where self-criticism cowered" (32). His self-imposed guilt over publication of Aubyn's love letters brought her back into his life more forcibly than if he had married her. Although distanced first by geography and later by death, Margaret Aubyn has achieved psychic omnipresence, a state more threatening to Glennard than physical proximity. He becomes furious without a reasonable object for his rage.

> Anger against whom? . . . against that mute memory to which his own act had suddenly given a voice of accusation? Yes, that was it; and his punishment henceforth would be the presence, the inescapable presence, of the woman he had so persistently evaded. She would always be there now. It was as though he had married her instead of the other. It was what she had always wanted—to be with him—and she had gained her point at last. (32)

Glennard's initiation into sin alters his perception of personal relationships past and present, making him distrust himself and others. "Losing all sense of proportion where the *Letters* were concerned" (54), he begins to perceive everything as pointing to them and to his moral lapse. When virtually in the depths of despair, he sees in a magazine photograph of Margaret Aubyn, now dead, the femininity that had evaded him in living contact. That which was

> feminine in her, the quality he had always missed, stole towards him from her unreproachful gaze; and now that it was too late, life had developed in him the subtler perceptions which could detect it in even this poor semblance of herself. . . .
> Then a sense of shame rushed over him. . . . The shame was deep, but it was a renovating anguish; he was like a man whom intolerable pain has roused from the creeping lethargy of death. (61)

"Renovating anguish" and new perceptions arise from "the mere abstraction of a woman" found in a dim photograph. This disembodied image serves as transition from the maternal imago to a more realistic picture of the woman herself. As an abstraction from life, the photo is frozen and immutable, but vague enough to stir up memory and revive imagination. This movement cracks through his emotional stasis by rendering the imago susceptible to modification and preparing his soul for change.

Glennard arose the next day feeling spiritually revived, with a sense of Aubyn's nearness now become "the one reality in a world of shadows." He reexperiences their past in memory, at last prepared to reinterpret its meaning "like a man who has mastered the spirit of a foreign tongue" (61). However, he is now subject to remorse for failing to appreciate Aubyn while she was alive. The renewal process has only begun; there is more work to do.

Having avoided Aubyn's funeral, he must confront the reality of her death by visiting her grave for the first time. Here his first reaction is an esthetic one—what a hideous final dwelling place for this artistic woman! But he recovers his pious mood and experiences for an exalted moment amidst the odor of decaying flowers the presence of Aubyn's spirit, "not the imponderable presence of his inner vision, but a life that beat warm in his arms" (64). He has brought her back into a guilt-free intermediate region in which change can occur.

He can now benefit from the continuities between his first woman and his wife. Early in the story Glennard had placed Alexa's picture in the same silver frame where Aubyn's had "long throned," replacing one with the other but also recognizing their congruence. The women are counter-images of each other. Margaret Aubyn, like her creator, was a woman of the word—aggressively so, in that she not only spoke audaciously but made a successful literary career. The passive Alexa Trent spoke little, rarely read anything, and seldom wrote letters of more than one page (21). A woman of "smiling receptivity" and few requirements, Alexa could sit with folded hands and wait for the movements of her husband's spirit. She preferred to leave troubling matters unspoken and resisted Glennard's requests for explanations.

To Glennard's astonishment, Alexa feels pity and love for poor neglected Margaret rather than the jealousy he expected. Alexa, the non-reader, insisted on reading precisely the book that her husband wished her to avoid, Aubyn's letters to himself. The two contrasted women reside in Glennard's psyche as polarities or complementarities. The first woman made possible his marriage to the second, and the second rescued the memory of the first, helping him refashion Margaret's memory into a usable past.

The theme of money running through "The Touchstone" stands for a base metal that awaits transmutation into gold. Margaret Aubyn's love, although experienced as tyrannical, provided a heritage that Glennard would eventually convert into usable currency. On the practical level, her letters funded his marriage, and, as her imperishable gift to him, they became the inheritance that he would either squander or invest. Of love and letters Aubyn gave liberally with little return. Glennard learns that

> he stood for the venture on which Mrs. Aubyn had irretrievably staked her all. . . . they might have stood for thrift and improvidence in an allegory of the affections.
>
> It was not that Mrs. Aubyn permitted herself to be a pensioner on his bounty. . . . She had no wish to keep herself alive on the small change of his sentiment; she simply fed on her own funded passion, and the luxuries it allowed her made him, even then, dimly aware that she had the secret of an inexhaustible alchemy. (13)

Even of her literary gifts Aubyn was lavish, squandering "her rarest vintage" in letters to him. He found such prodigality oppressive when he was tempted to sell the letters:

> He was almost frightened now at the wealth in his hands; the obligation of her love had never weighed on him like this gift of her imagination; it was as though he had accepted from her

something to which even a reciprocal tenderness could not have justified his claim. . . . [Suddenly realizing that the letters could "fund" his marriage] he could almost fancy some alchemistic process changing them to gold as he stared. (15)

The temptation was a reverse alchemy that would debase to utilitarian purposes the high gift of a woman's imagination. But Aubyn's gift of imagination contained the seed of its own ultimate reversal. It lay dormant awaiting Glennard's need, enabling him eventually to convert neurotic guilt into a manageable sense of ordinary forgivable human sin. But not without suffering.

By giving without stint and allowing Glennard to exploit her, Aubyn had generated in him a guilt so oppressive that only after severe penance could he accept forgiveness. At first Alexa is too prompt with compassion; her ready forgiveness for his sale of the letters fails to meet his need for atonement. He says:

> "Don't you see that it's become an obsession with me? That if I could strip myself down to the last lie—only there'd always be another one left under it!—and do penance naked in the marketplace, I should at least have the relief of easing one anguish by another? Don't you see that the worst of my torture is the impossibility of such amends?" (80)

Glennard demands punishment from a woman, one who can judge as well as forgive, who can provide cleansing antisepsis as well as healing balm. In his festering moral anguish Glennard craves the sting of Alexa's scorn, "since her contempt would be a refuge from his own," very much like a child demanding punishment from his mother:

> What he wanted now was not immunity but castigation: his wife's indignation might still reconcile him to himself. Therein lay his one hope of regeneration; her scorn was the moral antiseptic that he needed, her comprehension the one balm that could heal him. (55)

Alexa's mediation guides Glennard through the conversion process. Her assumption of his burden made him feel "like a child coming back to the sense of an enveloping presence; her nearness was a breast on which he leaned" (78). With her help, the internalized Aubyn was transformed from one of the punitive Furies or Erinyes to one of the gracious Eumenides. In the fullness of time, after months of grinding anguish, he was released from the dead woman's terrible grip and enabled to reincorporate her into his psychic system as a blessing. With this much emphasis on confession of sin and female intercession the tale suggests a yearning on Wharton's part to move from a deterministic Calvinistic ethos to a Catholic one offering the hope of absolution from sin.[4]

The "great renewal" of the finale occurs gradually, like a spring thaw or like "laboriously learning the rudiments of a new language." Glennard has to grope for a correct view of Alexa "through the dense fog of his humiliation" (78). At the climactic moment, she helps him to a spiritual "turning" by offering a re-conception of his act—enlarging it from neurotic self-imposed guilt that bores ever inward to the broader concept of human sin, for which traditional remedies are available. Alexa's revisioning of Glennard's act, "an immense redistribution of meanings" (77), becomes the moral touchstone that allows him to perceive and acknowledge the true gold bequeathed him by Margaret Aubyn.

Like a good therapist, Alexa modifies Glennard's desperate fear of being a permanently doomed sinner by offering him the analogy of early Christians who purified rather than destroyed heathen temples. This transformational viewpoint allows him to eliminate the negative aspects of the Aubyn relationship and salvage the beneficial ones. His sexual resistance to the mother-figure, the unrecompensed benefits he took from her, his virtual destruction of her—are all in the nature of things, stages in achieving full adulthood. He says gropingly:

> She wished the best for me so often, and now, at last, it's through her that it's come to me. But for her I shouldn't have known you—it's through her that I've found you.... I took everything from her—everything—even to the poor shelter of loyalty she's trusted in—the only thing I *could* have left her! I

took everything from her, I deceived her, I despoiled her—and she's given me *you* in return! (81–82)

Alexa replies that Margaret Aubyn's sacrifice did not, as he thought, give him a wife, but rather gave him back to himself that he might become a real husband, thus lifting Glennard's burden of indebtedness. Because Aubyn's best recompense was the joy of giving (82), he need feel no guilt. Having destroyed and repaired the mother-figure, Glennard can now re-establish his marriage. The couple will progress from sojourning in a fragile holiday tent to dwelling in a sturdy, durable home.

◆   ◆   ◆

By fusing a redemptive religious element with the psychological and the sexual, Wharton added the hope of grace and salvation to what otherwise must have seemed like psychic entrapment. In her own life, the triple nexus occurred early— in her childhood view of her mother as simultaneously an inscrutable Calvinist God and the super-ego that censored her thoughts and seemed to demand complete denial of the child's sexuality.

The needy child in Wharton saw herself as Stephen Glennard, who eventually learned to take from Margaret Aubyn what he required to assuage his anguish and to salvage his life. Lacking the kind of mothering she craved, Wharton substituted a vision of herself as provider of nurturance. This strategy is somewhat like that of elder daughters in motherless families who, deprived of nurturance themselves, bask vicariously in the maternal care they provide for younger siblings. Prominent in Wharton's childhood memories was a small furry dog, recipient of young Edith's tenderest empathic imagination. Reincarnations of Foxy were to accompany Wharton throughout life, pampered to the point of irritating less animal-infatuated friends. By assuming a maternal role with respect to small dogs, she could bring a measure of maternal solicitude under her own control, make sure that it was present in her world, and then identify with the recipient of this, her own tenderness. Later in life she assumed a maternal posture toward Morton Fullerton, her lover, and following that toward other young men in her social circle.

About seven years after publication of "The Touchstone," the semi-maternal relationship between Margaret Aubyn and Glennard functioned as a paradigm for Edith Wharton's relationship to Morton Fullerton. In both life and fiction the older woman gave more than she received and in both she made of her relationship to a callow man a high imaginative experience.

SEXUAL AWAKENING IN MID-LIFE: THE FULLERTON AFFAIR

> "She felt like a slave, and a goddess, and a girl in her teens."
>
> *The Reef*

When Henry James introduced Morton Fullerton to Edith Wharton in the fall of 1907, Fullerton was forty-two years old, she was forty-five and an established writer. She was preparing herself to shed an unsatisfactory marriage of more than twenty years and hoping for a last opportunity to experience love. By this time her need for profound emotional experience outweighed her disapproval of adultery and divorce. Feeling emotionally stagnant, her soul seemed to demand the tumultuous upheaval of passion. Even more than most women, and in more than just a physical way, she required what psychologist Sophie Freud calls "the passion experience," a focusing of all the psychic energies on a single point, on something or someone outside the self.[5] At the time of their meeting, Morton Fullerton had broken up a brief marriage with a French singer, had become engaged to his adoptive sister Katharine, and was probably frightened by this strange development. With a childless married woman such as Edith Wharton, he could indulge his predilection for familial eroticism without risk of commitment. The friendship quickly flowered into an intensely passionate love affair for some months following Wharton's move to Paris in 1908.

Morton Fullerton has a bad reputation with Wharton's admirers. Leon Edel calls him variously "an elegant seducer," a "libertine," and a "middle-aged mustached Lothario." R. W. B. Lewis, Wharton's biographer, refers in his edition of her letters to Fullerton's "smiling selfishness" and "sheer slackness of nature." Although generally characterized as a rotter and a scoundrel, Fullerton liberated the sexuality of some remarkably discerning men and women. Furthermore, he was magnetic enough to retain their loyalty even after they learned that they were only a passing phase in his gaudy sexual history. To each he gave the sensation of a unique, transcendent love for a brief period, then moved on to the next. Few ever turned away from this "dashing well-tailored man with large Victorian moustaches and languid eyes, a bright flower in his button-hole, and the style of a 'masher'."[6]

Such was the ripened Fullerton whom biographer Leon Edel met in Paris, an expatriate from a provincial New England ministerial home who had been a brilliant success at Harvard and gone on to a journalistic career as the Paris representative of the London *Times*. Successful also in literary circles, he was a friend of George Santayana, Bernard Berenson, Henry James, and Oscar Wilde.

To those who perceived the scoundrel and masher in Fullerton, the idea that he could have been the lover of Edith Wharton seemed so improbable that for years biographers assumed that the man addressed in her torrid "Love Diary"[7] was the genteel diplomat Walter Berry. Although she did indeed have great love for Berry, she may well have publicized that fact in her memoir, *A Backward Glance*, as a red herring to throw people off Fullerton's scent.[8]

Wishing that there be no record of the affair, she returned or destroyed Fullerton's letters and begged him to do likewise with hers. Ignoring her repeated demands, he preserved hundreds of her letters, which are now open to public scrutiny just as she feared. He tended to hold on to letters even though some of them had already led to threats of blackmail. At one point Wharton and Henry James helped him raise money to buy off a mistress, Henrietta Mirecourt, who threatened him with compromising letters she had found from Lord Gower and others from Margaret Brooke, the Ranee of Sarawak. In his needy old age Fullerton still had on hand letters from Henry James, which he sold to raise funds.[9]

Edith Wharton's passion for William Morton Fullerton is a mystery in the story of her life and a fascinating puzzle in the psychology of love. The recent emergence of hundreds of love letters she wrote to him (now in the archives of the University of Texas at Austin) intensifies rather than resolves the question of why she chose a chronically faithless man who was also bisexual. To probe the question of her choice we must ask why this particular man was able to release her long-imprisoned sensuality. Why did this moralistic woman yield so readily to an adulterous liaison, and why with a man whose sexual history and personal style pointed so clearly toward her ultimate humiliation? Beyond the obvious answers of age, need, and opportunity, we find a curious matching at the deeper levels of personality.

In Chapter 1 we saw indications of a secret sexual life that young Edith was able to pursue outside of direct maternal surveillance. By giving up normal expressions of sexual curiosity, she permitted herself a florid fantasy life that probably included incestuous elements and may have led to self-stimulation. Given her sense of maternal omniscience, she must have felt that she was being observed even in the "secret garden" of her fantasy, and judged herself guilty for enjoying substitute forms of eroticism. If the outer mother was deceived by Edith's renunciations, the inner one, that Calvinistic god of her own creating, was not. She would have to atone for her hidden pleasures, so that sexuality would never be possible for her without an element of guilt and punishment. This accords with the perverse strategy that psychoanalyst Louise J. Kaplan finds characteristic of sexually submissive women, a strategy designed to atone for unconscious guilt with conscious torment. Wharton's adult eroticism, according to Kaplan, "could flourish only in a forbidden relationship where sin and guilt were conscious," i.e., in an adulterous relationship into which was built an element of self-abasement.

Kaplan regards the Fullerton affair not as a grand passion but as a form of perversion, because of Wharton's "insistence on her worthlessness and her willingness to accept his tyranny."[10] Viewing this position as an unconsciously chosen sexual bondage, Kaplan observes: "When this subservience and submissive dependency on an idealized authority, an attitude typical of a young child toward the parents, becomes a pronounced feature of an adult relationship, it is tantamount to perversion."[11] In placing herself at the mercy of a man she herself had endowed with dominance, Wharton was, according to this theory, reenacting a childhood sense of maternal abandonment, with the added element of partial control. The lover "becomes invested with tyranthood by virtue of his physical and emotional comings and goings, which are interpreted as a giving of love and a taking away of love. In extreme submissiveness the erotic desire is not directed toward an actual person but rather toward a situation of tyranny. . . . The threat of abandonment is an essential ingredient of a perverse script."[12] Kaplan concludes, however, that unlike other slaves to submissive love, Wharton was able eventually to extricate herself sufficiently to regain her own autonomy.

◆　　◆　　◆

With this picture in mind, we turn to Morton Fullerton—asking first and especially the nature and origins of his amatory style, which was appealing enough to awaken the repressed eroticism of such disciplined celibates as Edith Wharton and Henry James. Addressing the puzzle of Fullerton's appeal to such people, R. W. B. Lewis describes Fullerton's "dreamy vein of idealism" and his "inherited interest in religious matters: meditations on proofs of the existence of God alternated in his pocket diary with references to politics, literature, and art. But religious idealism mingled in Morton

Fullerton's make-up with a no less positively marked erotic impulse and a strong sexual appeal."[13] Fullerton's ability to fuse the religious with the erotic, even his libertinism, can be understood with reference to ideas current in turn-of-the-century artistic circles.

But to understand the lasting appeal of this emotionally exploitative man to morally discerning people requires another kind of inquiry. We must look to the origin of Morton Fullerton's affective life in his relationship to his mother, then to the extension of this to his adopted sister, and thence to an oddly diverse series of lovers. Few ever rejected him on ethical grounds; even Camille Chabert, the French wife he put aside shortly after she bore his child, remained obsessed with him for the rest of her life.[14]

The mustachioed libertine who was to arouse Wharton's slumbering sensuality had performed a similar role, according to Leon Edel, in the erotic life of Henry James. Edel places Morton Fullerton at the very center of James's awakening to homoerotic feelings, treating the encounter of the fifty-year-old celibate author with the young journalist as the opening wedge of a series of such late-life involvements.

The letters James wrote to Fullerton are undoubtedly love letters despite their ostentatiously hyperbolic tone. Thanking Fullerton for a letter, James wrote:

> How, my dear Fullerton, *does* a man write in the teeth of so straight a blast from—I scarce know what to call the quarter: the spice-scented tropic isles of Eden—isles of gold—isles of superlative goodness? I have told you before that the imposition of hands in a certain tender way "finishes" me, simply— and behold me accordingly more finished than the most *parachevé* of my own productions. . . . You do with me what you will . . . You're at any rate the highest luxury I can conceive, and . . . I should wonder how the devil I can afford you. However, I shall persist in you. I know but this life. I want in fact more of you. . . . You are dazzling, my dear Fullerton; you are beautiful; you are more than tactful, you are tenderly, magically *tactile*. (September 26, 1900)

In 1907 he asked, "*Can* one man be as mortally, as tenderly attached to another as I am to you?" As in his letters about Wharton calling her an "Angel of Devastation," James dared to express genuine feelings under a mask of playful exaggeration. And like Fullerton's mother earlier and Edith Wharton later, James often sounded the wistful cry, "I want more of you!" Fullerton gave of himself intensely in brief encounters, but knew the value of making himself scarce.

Paradoxically, Morton Fullerton's own freedom from conventional constraints provided a model and a sanction for one so painfully inhibited as Wharton. She was delighted to experience at last "what happy women know," even though aware from the start that it would not last and would ultimately prove painful. She was ready for what Sophie Freud's research on women who first experience overpowering love in middle life defines as "the passion experience." Most of her subjects would endorse the following words from one of them who first experienced passion in her forties: "No matter that it ends in sadness because for a little while I've been in touch with what feels like the kernel of my soul."[15]

Fullerton, an experienced sensualist of eclectic appetites, would not long rest satisfied with an older married woman of little beauty who was also his senior in professional accomplishment. Indeed, she was to learn that he could not long rest satisfied with anyone regardless of age or appearance. Even from the beginning she prepared herself for the inevitable termination of the passionate side of the affair while trying to preserve other aspects of the relationship. Wharton maintained the connection through correspondence for the next thirty years, the duration of her life, despite Fullerton's dilatory responses.

Edith Wharton deluged her beloved with missives long after the passion died out, and like the letters of her fictitious novelist, Wharton's have become publicly accessible and many are now published, an eventuality that she dreaded.[16] Remembering her own novella about the posthumous publication of love letters, she frequently sounded the following note without success.

> Cher ami—Can you arrange, some day next week . . . to bring, or send, me such fragments of correspondence as still exist? I have asked you this once or twice, as you know. . . . My love of order makes me resent the way in which inanimate things survive their uses! (November 27, 1909)

His failure to comply did not stem the flow of her letters, and Fullerton was not one to destroy documents. He preserved letters from many of his lovers even after such records had caused him legal problems.

Wharton anticipated such behavior in "The Touchstone," which debates extensively the ethics of publishing private letters. Defenders of publication argue that "a personality as big as Margaret Aubyn's belongs to the world. . . . It's the penalty of greatness—one becomes a *monument historique*. Posterity pays the cost of keeping one up, but on condition that one is always open to the public" (38). Proponents of the right to privacy (who nevertheless devour the letters), exclaim "I believe it *is* a vice, almost, to read such a book. . . . It's the woman's soul, absolutely torn up by the roots—her whole self laid bare; and to a man who evidently didn't care. . . . They're unloved letters" (36–37).

Much that Wharton says about Aubyn's motives for pursuing Glennard with unsought missives helps explain the mystery of her own attachment to Morton Fullerton. "The Touchstone" portrays the special intimacy attainable through letters in the absence of physical proximity:

> Their friendship dragged on with halting renewals of sentiment, becoming more and more a banquet of empty dishes. [When they separated they] exchanged the faded pleasures of intercourse for the comparative novelty of correspondence. *Her letters, oddly enough, seemed at first to bring her nearer than her presence.* She had adopted . . . a note as affectionately impersonal as his own; she wrote ardently of her work, she questioned him about his. (12–13; italics added)

Wharton was to adopt just this kind of "affectionately impersonal" tone of professional banter when the affair descended from passion into camaraderie.

Paradoxically, Aubyn finally emigrated to Europe, leaving Glennard behind, in order, she said, to "see him always . . . to be nearer him" (14). Thereafter the current of her letters became a flood. Like Wharton in matters of the heart, Aubyn sees most intensely through the eye of imagination.[17] This conception of intimacy enhanced by distance helps explain why love letters provided Wharton an especially satisfying means of relationship.[18] Letters liberate the correspondents from mundane reality, giving fuller range to the imagination and permitting idealization of both partners. For a time, the Morton Fullerton of Wharton's imagination became her idealized "other self" as well as the mirror of the self she was yearning to liberate or create.[19]

The personalities generated in epistolary space could act out normally suppressed parts of the self, freeing them from domination by the public persona. Wharton had already prepared the way for this overthrow of conventional restraints by her reading in transcendental thinkers such as Whitman and Nietzsche, a tradition that Fullerton knew how to exploit in his sexual conquests. Good intellectual authority enabled her to build a bridge between religious and sexual antinomianism: "I feel as though all the mysticism in me, the transcendentalism that in other women turns to religion were poured into my feeling for you, giving me a sense of immanence, inseparableness from you" (April 2, 1908). Describing herself in "The Love Diary" as "Jenseits von Gut und Böse" ("beyond good and evil"), she threw herself into the religion of passion.

In letters to her lover, this proud, autonomous woman permitted herself to express long-denied emotional needs, to relinquish control and abandon the pose of self-sufficiency. Sometimes abasing herself to the point of begging for response, she marveled in "The Love Diary" that "I, who dominated life, stood aside from it so, how I am humbled, absorbed, without a shred of will or identity left! . . . How the personality I had moulded into such strong firm lines has crumbled to a pinch of ashes in this flame!" (April 20, 1908).

From these ashes emerged her long-suppressed passional self: "You woke me from a long lethargy, a dull acquiescence in conventional restrictions, a needless self-effacement. . . . all one side of me was asleep" (to Fullerton, August 26, 1908). Reveling in the marvel of this late awakening through which she overcame a lifetime of sexual and social inhibitions, she wrote of "throbbing pulses" and the "ripple of flame" stimulated by the mere sight of her lover (March 1908). During these first years of the affair, she composed and inscribed to Morton Fullerton erotic poems such as "Ogrin," celebrating the triumph of love over convention. After a particularly gaudy night at the Charing Cross Hotel in London, Wharton wrote the blank-verse poem "Terminus," which begins "Wonderful was the long secret night you gave me, my Lover," and then follows the spiritual-erotic communion to its conclusion: "And lying there hushed in your arms, as the waves of rapture receded. / And far down the margin of being we heard the low beat of the soul."[20]

The poem "Life," discussed above in Chapter 1, dramatizes an important aspect of Wharton's psychology—a yearning to be mastered by another, a situation that she could then transpose into her own form of domination. The reedpipe that had been rapt out of Lethean torpor by the female personification called Life expresses tremulous delight in being pierced into an instrument that will be played on by the god of love and then is so transported by ecstasy as to become the player rather than the instrument. The poem embodies swift alternations between dominance and submission, so that the precondition of rapture is to be rapt by another, whom the slave then proceeds to master. The reed merged with Life until "she became the flute and I the player. / and lo! the song I played on her was more / Than any she had drawn from me." As the reed finally says to Life, "thy bosom thrill / With the old subjection, then when Love and I / Held thee, and fashioned thee, and made thee dance / Like a slave-girl to her pipers."[21]

A pattern for this way of loving had been set much earlier in a poem written in Wharton's late teens that expressed her ideal of love:

> Ah, yes, to you I might have been
> That happy being past recall,
> The slave, the helpmeet, and the queen,—[22]

In the course of Wharton's entanglement with Morton Fullerton she was to play all three roles—a slave (the self-abasing woman grateful for any crumbs of love), a helpmeet (the professional comrade who gave tactful advice), and finally a queen who would master the limitations of the affair by transmuting it into priceless experience and art.[23]

After transports of apparent communion came humiliating neglect. Fullerton, as was his wont in love affairs, began to distance himself. We flinch to see this proud woman abasing herself before his sudden indifference, begging for response, endlessly explaining her motives, trying to find a tone and the magic words that would bind him to her:

> After nearly a month my frank tender of friendship remains unanswered. . . . My reason rejects the idea that a man like you, who has felt a warm sympathy for a woman like me, can suddenly . . . lose even a friendly regard for her, & discard the mere outward signs of consideration by which friendship speaks. (August 26, 1908)

> What you wish, apparently, is to take of my life the inmost & uttermost that a woman—a woman like me—can give, for an hour, now & then, when it suits you; & when the hour is over, to leave me out of your mind & out of your life as a man leaves the companion who had accorded him a transient distraction. I think I am worth more than that. (Winter 1910)

In this Wharton echoes her earlier characterization of Stephen Glennard of "The Touchstone," who "requited [Margaret Aubyn's] wonderful pages, her tragic outpourings of love, humility and pardon, with the scant phrases by which a man evades the vulgarest sentimental importunities" (5). Having thus envisioned and depicted a one-sided love, Wharton still chose a chronically faithless man, a bisexual with a marked preference for older women, who at the time of wooing her was engaged to his cousin and adoptive sister, Katharine Fullerton. Though Wharton did not know all this at first, her discoveries did little to diminish her attachment and may even have served to confirm it.

Wharton, like many of Morton Fullerton's lovers, provided virtually limitless forgiveness for his ethical and sexual lapses. She offered to him the kind of love she most craved for herself, unlimited acceptance despite recognition of faults. Although this one-sided love seems masochistic, it has its proud, autonomous element. Like Margaret Aubyn, Edith Wharton took responsibility to raise the crop for which the man had merely "supplied the seed." She "simply fed on her own funded passion" because, again like her character, "she had the secret of an inexhaustible alchemy" (13). This emotional and artistic alchemy that changes stones into bread, base metal into valuable currency, implies a covert mastery of self, man, and situation.

The relationship that Wharton anticipated in "The Touchstone" was fulfilled in life and then returned to literature in "The Mortal Lease," a sequence of love sonnets written during the affair that plays gravely with Fullerton's doctrine of the transcendental moment. After having complied with the doctrine for a while and experienced its transports, the speaker rejects the "sacramental cup" offered by the personified Moment, who flees, taunting the speaker that now she will never know whether the wine "globes not in every drop the cosmic show." The speaker retorts that her gift of imagination can amplify whatever she has kept from the experience: "I, that could always catch / The sunrise in one beam along the wall." In the final sonnet, she characterizes the lover's heart as a "velvet pliancy" that retains no image of passing experiences, in contrast to her own weary, scarred, and trampled heart, over which "a sacred caravan" moves "alone beneath the stars."[24] In the term "velvet pliancy" Wharton indicates that she had taken Fullerton's measure very early in the game, but that nevertheless he would serve her needs.

◆   ◆   ◆

Between this pair were emotional anomalies that dovetailed in odd ways. In the areas of maternal affection and sexual experience, Edith Wharton had been deprived, whereas Morton Fullerton had experienced excess. Wharton's early deprivation created a gap in her sense of being, a deficit to which she owed much of her shyness, fear of intimacy, and delayed sexual awakening. In an early letter to Fullerton Wharton wrote, using the economic metaphor that she often applied to the affections, of "the way you've spent your emotional life, while I've—bien malgré moi!—hoarded mine" (March 1908). Even at the height of her passion, the deprived hoarder was conscious that she had found in Fullerton a remedy for her inhibitions—a model and an authority for spending.

Morton Fullerton, on the other hand, had been almost smothered with maternal adoration. He was the older son of a poor and sickly New England minister and an intense, self-sacrificing mother with cultivated interests. His long residence in Europe as Paris correspondent for the *London Times* occasioned a great many letters from his mother and sister, allowing us a window into family relationships. Julia Fullerton was a worrier, a wife and mother who felt responsible for the solution of all family problems and burdened by this responsibility. She expected sympathy and admiration for her efforts, even for her intensity: "I sleep about four hours of the twentyfour . . . and the rest of the time my brain is active." Often she assumed a role of abused gallantry: "I smile tonight simply because it is my custom to smile on Sundays, but I am too tired."[25]

Although overinvolved with all her children, she took less pleasure in the adult children who lived nearby than in the distant one in Paris. William Morton Fullerton (Will, as the family called him) became the center of his mother's emotional life. In her letters, she turned to him for sympathetic understanding: "To whom can I go but you?"

> I shall never cease to be sad over the fate that took you away from me—It is cruel—It grows harder and harder for me to bear the separation. . . . Will, I want more of you. (February 26, 1899)

> Always the sense of loneliness comes over me at our separation, and the feeling that I must have you near. With a longing for you which can never be uttered. (October 1, 1899)

> You more than anyone else have the power to make me happy. . . . I long for you with such an intensity of feeling that it almost makes me sink from exhaustion sometimes—You are ever present with me.

> [Thank you for the gift of a bracelet.] I have a good deal of the feeling a young girl has when her lover makes her a gift.[26]

Although coy enough to speak like a lover, Julia Fullerton was practical with money and free with bracing advice about wholesome Christian living and the management of business affairs. He would give her "untold joy" if he would "leave off tobacco and retire early." She recommended less dissipation and told him how to extract more vacation time from his chief in the Paris branch of the *Times*. She followed the stock market closely and provided staunch advice about saving money (withdraw savings only in case of positive need) to this son in his forties.

In addition to such practical virtues, Julia Fullerton could converse with her son on literary and cultural matters. She wrote of the new archaeological "finds" in Egypt, shared her reactions to "Quo Vadis" and the works of Kipling, and discussed with Morton her planned addresses to her literary club. She even corrected his spelling, and in 1897, when he was a professional journalist, suggested that he shorten his sentences and guard against stylistic ambiguities. With the exception of smoking, spelling, and Christian pieties, Edith Wharton was later to reiterate much of this advice.

Fullerton apparently basked in his mother's adoration and

concern but feared engulfment. He failed to answer most of her letters, causing her to beg him for replies, for news, for response. "To have to beg for love is humiliating," she wrote in 1904. "I cannot conceive of a harder thing to bear than for parents who idolize a child to feel that they have become of very little importance to that child."[27] She became so desperate that Rob, her younger son, berated Morton for neglecting her feelings. In the mother-son relationship originated a lifelong affective pattern—pursuit and acceptance of female adoration while returning only enough to maintain the flow of love in his direction.

Fullerton came to depend on the advice and devotion of practical, strong-minded women. Although he eventually distanced himself from his mother by the width of the Atlantic, he transferred some of his oedipal feelings to his adoptive sister Katharine, who grew up believing herself to be his true sister. Born in 1879 and about fourteen years younger than Morton, Katharine regarded him as her intellectual mentor and soulmate. He encouraged her erotic feelings and indulged his own under protection of a literal but deceptive interpretation of the incest barrier.

When Katharine learned just before her twenty-fifth year that they were not brother and sister but cousins, she proclaimed her lifelong passion for him and desire to marry him.[28] She wrote to him on November 9, 1907: "Ah, my own, my own—You know that I am quite simply desperately in love with you: that in your own sacred words . . . 'without marriage there is no life for you nor for me.' " After Morton dissolved his brief marriage to a French woman, Camille Chabert, he and Katharine became engaged despite serious parental objections. The parents blamed Katharine for seducing Morton's affections; for the family's blindness and deception over the years they showed no sign of contrition. Fullerton kept Katharine dangling for several years without marrying her, at the same time carrying on the affair with Edith. After giving Morton one last opportunity to claim her, Katharine married Princeton University professor Gordon Gerould in 1910.[29]

Despite the self-abasement she displayed toward Morton, Katharine was a strong-minded, authoritative, and somewhat feisty woman. She taught English for many years at Bryn Mawr College and eventually became a successful writer of fiction, essays, and criticism (including laudatory and discerning commentaries on the work of Edith Wharton). Wharton even helped place Katharine's first novel, *Vain Oblations*, with Scribner's. In 1922, long after her marriage, Katharine published a story that presents a slightly disguised version of her relationship with Morton, "East of Eden" (collected in *Valiant Dust*).

All his life Fullerton had been playing with incestuous feelings in both directions, as a son toward his mother and as a father- and brother-figure toward his cousin. The overheated mother-son relationship was probably the source of his affair with a woman fifteen years older than himself, Margaret Brooke, the Ranee of Sarawak, as well as of the cruel game he played with Katharine's feelings. His engagement to Katharine narrowly skirted acting out his oedipal impulses within his own family. Over the years, Fullerton acquired considerable emotional versatility, a capacity to play variations on sexual roles, so that he would attract mother-figures and daughter-figures, men and women, and in general mentors to whom he could also teach a good deal by serving as a sexual liberator. Protean and amoral, he learned to alter the valence on his personal qualities, so that he could, for example, represent his self-indulgent weakness as a defiant refusal to play socially determined roles.

In terms of incest desires, Edith Wharton had yearned in imagination for much that Morton Fullerton flirted with acting out. Her interest in oedipal themes and father-daughter incest are pornographically revealed in the "Beatrice Palmato" fragment. This side of her responded to Fullerton's nimble games on the boundaries of incest. Her sense of conflict between a masculine professional identity and an ardent but stifled feminine self responded to Fullerton's alternating gender signals. He activated her repertory of repressed possibilities, she affirmed his versatility. He was languid, she tough and disciplined. He was the spender, she the hoarder. He initiated her sexually, and she mothered him in practical matters, mentored him in professional ones.

His protean qualities are reflected in two of the women who adored him. There were many temperamental and stylistic similarities between Katharine Fullerton and Edith Wharton. Both women needed to explain and analyze themselves to a percipient other and found in Morton Fullerton an "other self" in which to mirror the selves they were creating through words. That self, in both instances, was the noble, self-denying woman whose fulfillment consisted in helping her man to true self-realization, an essentially maternal posture if not that of the "slave" who is also a helpmeet and queen. At especially exalted moments both women offered to make no worldly claims for themselves, mutual love being the only bond worthy of their high-souled devotion.

Wharton often played the self-abnegating mother to which Fullerton was so long accustomed: "I could be the helpful comrade who walked beside you for a stretch & helped you carry your load. . . . But the last words of all, Dear, is that whatever you wish, I shall understand; I shall even understand your *not* understanding" (Ransom Center, n.d.). In a similar vein, Katharine depicted herself as secondary, subordinate in importance, ready to be whatever he needed. She asked only to be near him when he needed her, yet claimed to be "ready with equal cheerfulness, to leave you when I hindered."[30]

On November 9, 1907, just after her engagement to Morton and shortly after he met Edith Wharton, Katharine wrote: "For pain of yours I could kill myself in sorrow; for disaster that puts you beyond the reach of my service, I think I should kill myself. . . . I am but the sword in your hand, my darling: a shield to hold above your head. Use me: for you I am tempered steel." And in words that might have come from Wharton, Katharine wrote on November 22, 1907: "There is something hopelessly and finally humiliating about being so much at another person's mercy, but perfect love casteth out pride."

Such self-sacrificing pronouncements suggest that it is autonomous women who offer extravagant self-abnegation as their love gift. And Morton Fullerton had enough experience with his mother's assertive self-denial to fear the other edge of that tempered-steel sword.

Katharine wrote to Fullerton for the rest of her life, through marriage, motherhood, and grandmotherhood, without significant diminution of affection. In 1940, thirty years after her marriage, she wrote to Fullerton:

> I dream about you so often that it *must* prove I never, in my inmost consciousness, forget you. . . . My dreams of you are always happy; there is never a cloud between us and we are always going on, on, *not* saying goodbye. I think that malgré tout, you and I must always have been a little in love with each other.

Both lovers exalted the importance of his work, the older woman doing so through helpful criticism and the younger through rapt admiration. Since for a period they were writing to him concurrently, Fullerton could enjoy triple measures of the adoration and concern his mother was still serving up to him. Katharine yearned to be his helpmeet, to serve what she called the "immortal part of him," his work. Wharton, on the other hand, spoke as his professional senior and mentor. She urged for his book a "franker idiom" and manlier style without the "heavy tin draperies" of the *Times* jargon, and if he lacked models, she recommended Emerson, Froude, and Arnold (October 25, 1910).

Throughout the earlier years of her correspondence Wharton continually fortified her lover with bracing advice—how to be more manly, independent, and better disciplined. In one remarkable letter written near the height of their affair, she tells him how to wean himself from his dependency on the *Times* in order to "*recreate*" himself and "begin an independent existence." If he will only "form habits of systematic daily work" and cultivate relations with the right people, he will "*be* Morton Fullerton, at his best & fullest" (October 25, 1910). Repeatedly, she tried to teach him to favor long-range goals over immediate pleasures so that he might have better control over his life:

> Your inclination to make the most of each moment as it comes, & spend the "small change" of present pleasure to the last penny, perhaps inclines you more than you are aware to consider the risks of striking out for yourself & living laborious days. . . . You would *have* to do that with a certain austerity of purpose & resolution of will . . . & this interior discipline is exactly what I believe you need, & what would re-make your life & your personality if you accepted it now, for a few years, before you have *stiffened in a few habits.* (May 17, 1910)

The two women shared with Morton Fullerton the consciousness of a psychic division between the imaginative and the analytic faculties. Wharton wrote to him that he and she "are almost the only people . . . who feel the 'natural magic', au delà, dream-side of things, & yet need the netteté, the line—in thinking, in conduct—yes! in feeling too!" (June 8, 1908). Like Wharton, Katharine, too, felt such a division, could love extravagantly, but despised sentimentality, and often broke into French at emotional moments. She wrote to Fullerton near the time of their engagement that she hated equivocal situations, "J'aime les situations nettes."[31] Having lived the most equivocal of lives, Katharine became an anatomist of the ambiguous.

The combination of ardor, intellect, and intense personal morality inclined both the older and the younger woman to make a religion of love, elevating the erotic with the mystic. Morton Fullerton's rather self-serving transcendental code of love, applicable to a wide variety of situations, fueled the ardors of even less distinguished women than Edith Wharton and Katharine Fullerton.

For a sample of his amatory style we must rely on the few surviving love letters that he wrote to other women. To a "darling," probably Margaret Brooke, the Ranee of Sarawak, he wrote at two in the morning:

> The beauty, the safety of our love is our sensitiveness, our sense, our sanity; our lack of sentimentality, our deliberate

calm reckoning of the circumstances that have to do with it, that make it what it is, unique. We are both supremely intolerant of any laws that others make for us. We must create our own worlds. This may be sublimely, Satanically immoral, audaciously Promethean; but it is the way we are bound to live and be.... It came to me just now that we at last were so wise and free, though mutually enslaved, and that all the rest of the world were fools relatively to us in our happy condition as the chosen of the gods.[32]

Echoing these words, one of Fullerton's amours, who signed the letter with her nom de plume, Blanche Roosevelt, wrote to him, "I know no law not my own caprice and recognize no will not mine own volition. Yours I might bend to... but not easily."[33]

Wharton's grounding in the antinomian ideas of Whitman and Nietzsche had prepared the way for Fullerton's assault on the already-shaky citadel of her New York proprieties. Shrewdly using transcendental dogma in his other courtships, he played on established romantic notions of souls so elevated above conventional limitations that their love consecrates itself. By invoking a higher law, he spiritualized the carnal not only for himself but for those lovers who required elevated doctrine in order to free themselves from sexual inhibitions and taboos. Such an invocation spoke particularly to autonomous, high-minded, literary women such as Katharine Fullerton and Edith Wharton.

The ardent sexuality that Wharton could not express within marriage erupted with adolescent fury in an adulterous liaison. Freud's views on the role of the illicit in thawing a woman's frozen sensuality seem particularly relevant to the timing, the intensity, and the liberation of her mid-life extramarital affair:

The long abstinence from sexuality to which [women] are forced and the lingering of their sensuality in phantasy have in them, however, another important consequence. It is often not possible for them later on to undo the connection thus formed in their minds between sensual activities and something forbidden, and they turn out to be psychically impotent, i.e., frigid, when at last such activities do become permissible. This is the source of the desire in so many women to keep even legitimate relations secret for a time; and of the appearance of the capacity for normal sensation in others as soon as the condition of prohibition is restored by a secret intrigue— untrue to the husband, they can keep a second order of faith with the lover. . . . [Women] do not usually transgress the prohibition against sexual activities during the period of waiting, and thus they acquire this close association between the forbidden and the sexual.[34]

Circumstances had prepared Edith Wharton for a Morton Fullerton long before she met him. Like his other lovers, she found in him more than was really there, but something resembling her unmet needs. None of his women could build a home on Morton Fullerton's love, but each could construct around his polymorphous personality a shelter for her own homeless, placeless feelings.

Wharton's relationship to Fullerton was surely anguished, but it was not entirely negative. Although she sometimes complained that he treated their love like a "transient distraction," she always returned to his gift of "all imaginable joy." She wrote that "whatever those months were to you, to me they were a great gift, a wonderful enrichment; & still I rejoice & give thanks for them! You woke me from a great lethargy . . . a needless self-effacement" (August 26, 1908). This assessment resembles what one of Sophie Freud's clients reported about a late-life passion experience: "I had been depressed by feelings of mental and soul stagnation. The experience gave me a will to live. I will be eternally grateful to have known what it is/was to feel—really feel. The person who loved me brought me back to being a whole person—allowed me to be me—gave me back a feeling of worth. I am grateful for my life."[35]

Edith Wharton was determined to complete her human experience by pursuing at whatever age and at whatever cost her long-deferred sexual education. In her "summer before the dark," she was able to find in this shabby man "the thing best worth knowing" ("Love Diary," May 2, 1907). Despite the hurts and humiliations of the affair, she used it for her own development, turned it to creative uses. As she noted in a journal, "Ordinary troubles dry one up; they're as parching as the scirocco; but in every heart there should be one grief that is like a well in the desert."[36]

UNEXPECTED OBSTACLES: *THE REEF*

A dozen years after writing "The Touchstone," when her love affair had come and gone, Wharton was still weighing its significance. But now, with adultery behind her and contemplating divorce, she used fiction to reflect on the role of passion in human life. In *The Reef* (1912), a novel of mid-life love, she depicted a woman yearning to break out of her sexual inhibitions but ultimately unable to do so. "Unexpected obstacle," the sharp first words of the novel, foreshadows the reef of inhibitions hidden beneath the flood of Anna Leath's rising passion.

At the time Edith Wharton wrote *The Reef,* she was learning about her husband's flagrant infidelities after years of sexless marriage and coming to a new understanding of sexuality in men as well as in herself. It was shortly before their divorce, and she was taking in the meaning of their belated sexual adventures, the gratifying as well as the sordid aspects. At age fifty, even after the Fullerton affair, she still had much to learn. She continued her emotional education by revisiting her own acquired and almost invincible sexual ignorance in the character of Anna Leath.

This most Jamesian of Edith Wharton's novels centers on a claustrophobic group of four characters intensely occupied with reading each others' intentions. At its opening, a thirty-seven-year-old diplomat, George Darrow, is hastening from England to France to resume a lapsed relationship with his first love, Anna Leath, now a widow living in France with her young daughter and a grown stepson. At Dover, Darrow receives a brief telegram from Anna asking him to delay his visit to Givré, her French estate, because of an "unexpected obstacle." Very much chagrined to receive such a message while en route to Anna, he strikes up acquaintance with a vivacious young woman, Sophy Viner. While waiting in Paris for an explanation from Anna he spends a fortnight with Sophy, introducing the rapt and culturally deprived girl to the theater and sights of Paris. The two have a brief affair and part company. To Darrow it has been a pleasant interlude of little importance.

But months later, when he arrives at Givré to cement his engagement to Anna, he finds that Sophy has become her daughter's governess and is engaged to her stepson Owen Leath. Owen's grandmother opposes the match on grounds of class differences, but Anna, very much identified with and close to her stepson, promises the youth her support. Darrow knows Sophy's shabby social history and tries to protect her secrets, but cannot quite accept as a daughter-in-law a woman with whom he has had an affair. Caught in an ethical dilemma as well as an oedipal one, he equivocates with both women in the hope of directing Sophy away from his intended family without revealing his reasons.

Owen's correct perception that Sophy is still in love with Darrow reveals the underlying flaws in both prospective marriages. Sophy, preferring her idealized image of Darrow to an opportune marriage, renounces Owen and vanishes. But once Anna learns the truth, she is unable to commit herself to a man who had slept with Sophy while on his way to visit her. She becomes obsessed with lurid imaginings of their intimacies and vacillates at length between wanting the same for herself and regarding Darrow as tainted.[37] Unable to cross the threshold of passion, she finally dismisses Darrow and runs off in pursuit of Sophy, the woman who possesses the vital erotic secret. Sophy eludes her, and so, alas, does the clue to passional experience.

The Reef represents aspects of Wharton's love affair without the indiscretion of depicting a recognizable Morton Fullerton. At the time of composing the book, Wharton was showing sections of it to him for comments. George Darrow in no way shares Fullerton's tendency to transcendentalize love; he is an eager lover but always moderate and practical. Wharton borrows from her furtive meetings with Fullerton the tawdry atmosphere of the Terminus Hotel, where Sophy and Darrow come together. This shabby setting could, according to one's perspective, either cheapen an affair or lend it an aura of participating in common human experience. Wharton's poem "Terminus" celebrates the transcendence of squalor by democratic Whitmanian rapture. Sophy is able to retain a transcendent view of her entire affair, whereas Darrow comes to feel the cheapness of hotel love.

Despite deliberate differences, a subtle resemblance persists between Fullerton's and Darrow's attitudes. When Darrow is forced to recall the episode with Sophy he realizes that "he would have liked to be able to feel that, at the time at least, he had staked something more on it. . . . But the plain fact was that he hadn't spent a penny on it" (168). This is precisely the kind of economic metaphor in which Wharton had formerly written to Fullerton about his indifference.

The Reef utilizes primarily Fullerton's gift of sexuality as it affects the lives of two contrasting women. Sophy and Anna represent Wharton before and after the encounter with Fullerton, the repressed self and the self that finally experienced "what happy women know." Quite possibly Wharton realized by 1912 that she may have derived from Morton Fullerton more than was intrinsically there. Such a view is suggested by the tales under discussion in this chapter and by others ("The Letters," and "The Lamp of Psyche," for example) that represent women substantial enough to derive nourishment from "feeding on their own funded passion" in attachments to callow or inadequate men.

The *Reef* hints at the oedipal dimension of an intergenerational love knot but is more reticent about it than James's *Golden Bowl*, which it resembles in many ways. Anna Leath points at sexual infidelity as the horror that places Darrow

outside her pale, whereas what makes the two intended marriages genuinely impossible is that Anna would be marrying
the former lover of her stepson's wife, that Owen would have
married his stepfather-in-law's former mistress. Anna's dis-
missal of Darrow is also influenced by her overinvolvement in
her stepson Owen and her unconscious horror of sharing intimate knowledge of Darrow with Owen's intended wife Sophy.
Carnal knowledge crisscrossing these generational boundaries would make family life too claustrophobic for comfort.
The drama that Darrow had selected for Sophy's introduction
to Paris theater was *Oedipe*.

The Vital Secret

In *The Reef* as in "The Touchstone" Edith Wharton split aspects of herself between paired female counterparts. Anna
Leath plays the sexually repressed woman Edith Wharton
once feared she might remain. The part of Wharton that dared
convention to seize her moment with Morton Fullerton is
played by Sophy Viner, who possesses the "vital secret" of
erotic energy. In this novel one part of the composite woman
is in pursuit of the other. Unfortunately, Anna cannot hold on
to the part of herself she has disowned for too many years.

Both women in love with Darrow are in need of a secure
home. Sophy drifts from one sponsor to another. Anna is a
young widow about to be displaced from her French estate by
her stepson's marriage and needs a life partner and another
home. Echoing the "gay holiday tent" of "The Touchstone" as
a symbol of temporary shelter is the umbrella imagery of *The
Reef*. Both Sophy and Anna make their first appearances in
the novel under a cloth shelter, the one a *parapluie*, the other a
parasol. Darrow meets Sophy when he offers her protection
under his umbrella after her own had become inverted during
a rainstorm. Sophy accepts with alacrity and allows Darrow
to extend his protection beyond the flimsy umbrella to ten
days of pleasure, culture, and love in Paris. An improviser in
life, she can enjoy a collapsible shelter when she likes the man

who holds it over her head. In contrast, Anna Leath first appears sheltering herself from sunshine under a parasol at Givré (81), seeking protection from light and joy in order to preserve her ladylike complexion.

When pleased with Darrow, both women are willing to share his umbrella, and at critical points both decline the privilege. Refusing his offer of temporary shelter during a downpour, Anna ultimately excludes the possibility of a permanent one. Finally, somewhat like Fullerton, Darrow provides enduring shelter for neither Anna nor Sophy, a conclusion more cynical and world-weary than that of the more youthful, optimistic story "Touchstone." Sophy can do without Darrow's shelter, and Anna is not ready for it.

Unlike critics who feel they must choose between Anna and Sophy as bearers of the novel's message, I find it more useful to view these two women as mutually defining complementarities.[38] Like Margaret Aubyn and Alexa, Anna and Sophy are characterized by opposition on issues central to Wharton's interest. Sophy's background is vaguely déclassé. Anna's girlhood is a caricature of Wharton's, governed by an ideal of total emotional restraint and the "code of moral probity":

> In the well-regulated well-fed Summers world the unusual was regarded as either immoral or ill-bred, and people with emotions were not visited. . . . In a community composed entirely of people like her parents and her parents' friends she did not see how the magnificent things one read about could ever have happened. She was sure that if anything of the kind had occurred in her immediate circle her mother would have consulted the family clergyman, and her father perhaps even have rung up the police. (85)

But inwardly Anna knew that her perceptions of social restraint were exaggerated; girls of her class who did not share such views enjoyed life, married, and prospered. "She perceived, indeed, that other girls, leading outwardly the same life as herself . . . were yet possessed of some vital secret which escaped her. . . . They were wider awake than she, more alert, and surer of their wants" (85–86). She observed the way flirtatious girls of her own circle aroused men and wanted to try doing this herself but was prevented by some unknown obstacle. Feeling that she was experiencing life through a veil of unreality, she tried to break out by marrying. But she chose as her husband a dessicated collector of snuff boxes and was bewildered to find her emotional torpor unrelieved. Even after marriage and motherhood, this polished product of New York society remained sexually naive and emotionally virginal. When she meets Darrow again after the death of her husband and finds him still interested, she thinks that at last Prince Charming will awaken the sleeping beauty in her. But she underestimates the power of her ingrained psychic obstacles.

The reef on which her hopes founder is her suppressed self in the form of Sophy Viner, a young woman directly in touch with her desires. Sophy, who is spontaneous and lives for the moment, describes herself as "all for self-development and the chance to live one's life" (61). She is indeed impulsive, responsive, histrionic—oriented to the immediate and the actual. Less refined and cultured than Anna, even somewhat inarticulate, Sophy is close to and honors her own feelings. This governess of indeterminate social position is a woman in touch with herself, with the vital principle, with life.

No wonder that when Anna finds herself on the threshold of passion she looks to Sophy for guidance. While still ignorant of Sophy's previous affair with Darrow, she wants to keep the girl near her by promoting Sophy's match with Owen despite their obvious incongruities of social class. When Anna claims that this match is a precondition of her own marriage to Darrow, she overrides class barriers that so conservative a woman would normally have respected. Although she offers the vaguely noble reason of wanting Owen to enjoy happiness as great as her own, she clearly needs to keep this girl in the family. In order to emerge from layers of repression, her passional self needs Sophy's reinforcement. Sophy embodies the erotic principle that Anna had long before sacrificed to a false ideal of ladylike restraint and intellectual distancing. This governess is needed to lead into sexual maturity a grown woman who had passed through marriage and motherhood without experiencing passion.

Like the ardent young Edith Wharton, Anna had renounced her sexuality in favor of words and ideas. Whenever, in their first and youthful love, Darrow had tried to kiss Anna, she "wanted to talk to him about books and pictures, and have him insinuate the eternal theme of their love. . . . [She] flew her little kites of erudition, while hot and cold waves swept over her" (87). Verbally fluent, Anna was always distanced from her own very real ardor. Now in early middle age, with a last chance to experience love, she is split off from a part of herself that she very much wishes to recover. But postponement has become a habit, and she uses the strategy of family obligations to sustain it.

Anna's telegram postponing Darrow's visit—"Unexpected obstacle. Please don't come till thirtieth"—is characteristic of her in that it subordinates Darrow to family matters and postpones engagement with him. The ego ideal of responsibility serves as an excuse to avoid the fulfillment that tantalizes and terrifies her. Sophy, in contrast, readily defers her own plans so she can be with Darrow. She is open to opportunity, lives for the moment, and considering her financial need, acts fairly irresponsibly. We see no sign, however, that Sophy takes her opportunities at the expense of others. Although she is rather inarticulate, Darrow underestimates her when he concludes that "remoter imaginative issues" were beyond her, that there were no "echoes in her soul" (61). She proves at the last to have the highest imagination and perhaps the noblest soul of them all.

Except for its impingement on his matrimonial plans, Darrow thinks little of his diversion with Sophy during a lonely interval. But Anna, like Oedipus, whose name was evoked early in the book, relentlessly pursues every detail of this event. Knowing that her obsessive pursuit of his private life during the time that she had let him down was unraveling her marriage plans, she cannot stop herself. On the one hand she would like to shut out the facts, but "at the same time she was tormented by the desire to know more, to understand better, to feel herself less ignorant and inexpert in matters which made so much of the stuff of human experience" (294).

> And suddenly she was filled with anger at her blindness, and then at her disastrous attempt to see. Why had she forced the truth out of Darrow? . . . But she had probed, insisted, cross-examined, not rested till she had dragged the secret to the light. She was one of the luckless women who always have the wrong audacities. . . . She recoiled from her thoughts as if with a sense of demoniac possession. (322)

Beginning to feel exasperated by Anna's excessive vacillations and scruples, Darrow asks, "Is it anything to be proud of, to know so little of the strings that pull us? If you knew a little more, I could tell you how such things happen without offending you; and perhaps you'd listen without condemning me" (316).

Starting to understand, Anna "discerned for the first time instincts and desires, which, mute and unmarked, had gone to and fro in the dim passages of her mind, and now hailed each other with a cry of mutiny" (316–17). She remembers that she had been a cold wife to Fraser Leath, and that he had sought consolation in certain back streets of Paris. Perhaps this is how men are, she thinks, and Darrow might be forgiven. She vacillates madly between rejecting Darrow for uncleanness and wishing to imagine with ever greater clarity the details of his transgression. She wants to despise the participants and yet to experience at Darrow's hands what Sophy had experienced.

Darrow's personal possessions in his room at Givré give Anna a feeling of cozy intimacy until she recalls that "this is what Sophy Viner knew":

> And with a torturing precision she pictured them alone in such a scene . . . Had he taken the girl to an hotel . . . where did people go in such cases? Wherever they were the silence of the night had been around them, and the things he used had been strewn about the room . . . *Anna, ashamed of dwelling on the detested vision, stood up with a confused impulse of flight; then a wave of contrary feeling arrested her and she paused with lowered head.* (342; italics added; ellipses in original text)

When eventually Anna is forced to give up her too-long-protected innocence and recognize the "dark places" in her own bosom that she would "always have to traverse . . . to reach the beings she loved best" (353), she is left alone "in the desert of a sorrow without memories" (302). Her belated education has left her terrified by partial insights and lurid visions. She concludes with anguish, "I shall never know what that girl has known" (296).

She has split the man who erred from the man she loved. Intellectually, she comprehends that the good Darrow and the bad one were one person—a human being with much to offer her, and she tries to accept him. But at a deeper level she vacillates between alternating visions of the radically split image. Unable to bring together the two ways of seeing, she can only reject the torturing double vision. "But now she had begun to understand that the two men were really one. The Darrow she worshipped was inseparable from the Darrow she abhorred; and the inevitable conclusion was that both must go" (302).

Despite this loss, Anna gains something valuable from her costly experience:

> She seemed to herself to have passed through some fiery initiation from which she had emerged seared and quivering, but clutching to her breast a magic talisman. Sophy Viner had cried out to her: "Some day you'll know!" and Darrow had used the same words. They meant, she supposed, that when she had explored the intricacies and darknesses of her own heart her judgment of others would be less absolute. Well, she knew now . . . the deep discord and still deeper complicities between what thought in her and what blindly wanted. (319–20)

On ideological lines, connoisseurs of "renunciation" admire or condemn Anna Leath's final refusal to marry Darrow, but few comment on Sophy's renunciation of the opportunity to marry Anna's stepson Owen. Sophy renounces this socially and financially desirable match in order to cherish her own small flame for George Darrow. Sophy takes high ground in her renunciation of both Owen and Darrow, arguing for the Darrow of her imagination, which will be untouched by his

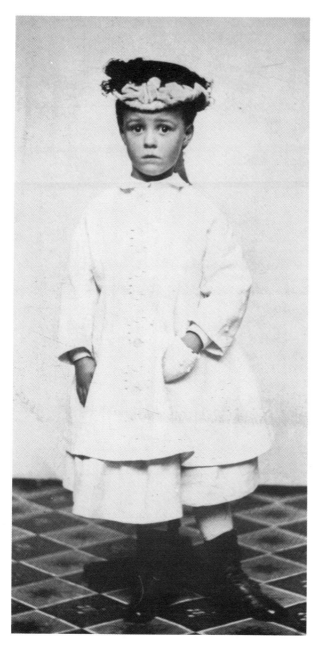

Edith Newbold Jones, age five. Permission, Edith Wharton estate.

Opposite, above: Edith's mother, Lucretia Rhinelander
Jones. Courtesy, Louis Auchincloss. Opposite, below:
Edith's father, George Frederic Jones. Courtesy,
Beinecke Library, Yale University. Above: Edith's nanny,
Hannah Doyle. Courtesy, Beinecke Library, Yale
University.

Edith's lover, William Morton Fullerton. Courtesy,
Beinecke Library, Yale University.

Edith's husband, Edward Robbins (Teddy) Wharton.
Courtesy, Beinecke Library, Yale University.

Edith's close friend and adviser, Walter Van Rensselaer Berry, circa 1905. Permission, Edith Wharton estate.

Edith Wharton, 1925. Courtesy, Lilly Library, Indiana University.

Edith Wharton, seated, and Catherine Gross at Ste. Claire le Chateau. Courtesy, Lilly Library, Indiana University.

expected marriage to Anna. Sophy says that she does not regret her fling with him because she will always have Darrow to herself to cherish in her own way, an inner possession untainted by how little the brief affair or she herself had meant to him. Finally, even Anna realizes that "Sophy Viner had chosen the better part, and that certain renunciations might enrich where possession would have left a desert" (334).

Sophy compares her own dedicated way of loving to a man's casual slaking of his sex drive but accepts the difference. She says,

> "I wonder what your feeling for me was? . . . Is it like taking a drink when you're thirsty? . . . I used to feel as if all of me was in the palm of your hand. . . . Don't think for a minute I'm sorry! It was worth every penny it cost. . . . I'd always wanted adventures, and you'd given me one, and I tried to take your attitude about it, to 'play the game' and convince myself that I hadn't risked any more on it than you. Then, when I met you again, I suddenly saw that I *had* risked more, but that I'd won more, too—such worlds! . . . I've made my choice—that's all: I've had you and I mean to keep you. . . . To keep you hidden away here," she ended, and put her hand upon her breast. (262–63)

What was casual to Darrow, Sophy makes into something of her own. Her idealism in this matches that of Margaret Aubyn and outstrips that of Anna Leath. It speaks, I believe, in the voice of Edith Wharton's unique form of autonomy—that of her mind and imagination, which could convert flawed experience into the nourishment she required.

Without the Fullerton experience, Wharton might have remained forever like Anna, married but virginal, yearning for a "fiery initiation" (319) but always cowering on the threshold. Instead, like Sophy, Wharton grasped what life offered, even though this connoisseur of fine environments had often to accept it in squalid station hotels with a man who did not keep her exclusively or even primarily in mind. She risked a great deal on this adventure, paid a high price in humiliation and anguish, but took away the valuable prize of the passion experience.

4

Parental Inscriptions

But the question is: *Which of us is her mother?*
The Old Maid

The Fullerton affair launched the richly productive period
that Cynthia Griffin Wolff calls Edith Wharton's "salamander" era, named for the mythical animal that could pass
through fire unscathed. In the works of this period, from *The
Reef* (1912) to *The Age of Innocence* (1920), Wharton at last
confronts the importance of human sexuality. On the personal
level, this era promised regeneration and delivered a good
measure of it, but the gain was not simple or constant. The
passion experience that Wharton had seized briefly at midlife
deepened her humanity, but such an isolated episode was not
sufficient to shelter her for a lifetime. Despite the variety and
number of male friends with whom she was to surround herself, Wharton continued to feel emotionally deprived. She had
neither a sexual partner nor a secure life companion—no one
who would effectively and reliably cherish her existence and
protect it from adversity. She had ameliorated her problem,
but not vanquished it.

THE COMPOSITE HUSBAND

Edith Wharton's marriage, mildly companionable at first but
never sexually fulfilling, became increasingly burdensome
with the passage of time. The more she developed as a writer

and intellectual the less companionship could she find with her husband Teddy. Kindly but perplexed, Teddy had difficulty finding a role for himself in the marriage. He wrote to Edith's friend Sally Norton of his pride in outfitting her automobile "with every known accessorie [sic] for comfort. You know I am no good on Puss's high plain of thought,—but you will agree that no lady of talent is as well turned out as she is."[1] Although proud of his wife, this amiable outdoorsman felt foolish among her sophisticated friends and generally excluded from the interests that drove her life. He seemed "positively frightened" by her literary work, almost convinced that "it was a kind of witchcraft."[2] Having no real work of his own, he was largely dependent on her income, much of it earned through her writing.

Coming to feel like a mere "passenger" in her fast-moving world, he became irascible and sometimes irresponsible. As his mental afflictions became more extreme, he openly flaunted his sexual adventures, which appear to date from the beginning of the Fullerton affair. Although Edith was pained and embarrassed by his flagrant disregard of appearances, as one who herself had strayed she tried to pass off his behavior with humor. On a motor trip with Daisy Chanler, Edith was signing into a hotel in a town that she had never before visited when she noticed an entry in the register, "Mr. and Mrs. Edward Wharton." She "observed with a slight smile and shrug: 'Evidently I *have* been here before.' "[3]

Sometimes, when Teddy had difficulty meeting the expenses of his mistresses, he helped himself to funds that Edith had entrusted to his care. Though irritated by his behavior, she felt compassion for his situation, as she revealed in a late summing-up: "There was no cruelty & no unkindness in him. Yet he was cruel & unkind through weakness."[4] She tried to find him effective psychiatric help, but increasingly the marriage seemed to her an intolerable prison. After years of painful consideration, she dissolved the twenty-eight year marriage by divorce under French law in 1913.

By this time she had created around herself a system of male companionship that functioned almost as a composite husband, although without provision for physical intimacy. Bernard Berenson's friendship came into Edith Wharton's life when Morton Fullerton was phasing out of it. With Berenson she shared intellectual and esthetic tastes and a love of travel. He became her ami or camerado, the companion of many a lively art and architectural tour, but could not give her the unequivocal admiration that she needed. Furthermore, he was married.

Gradually, she built around herself a society of intellectual young men—including, among others, Gaillard Lapsley, Howard Sturgis, Robert Norton, and Percy Lubbock. The group, generally known as the Qu'Acre set, found its physical center in Queens Acre, Howard Sturgis's home near Windsor in England. Along with Henry James the group formed a close circle of which Edith Wharton was the central female, a position that kept her feeling feminine and flirtatiously alive.

Despite her gaiety within this bachelor group, Percy Lubbock recognized her personal insecurity, her divided selfhood, and her essential loneliness:

> She liked to be surrounded by the suit of an attentive court, and she like to be talked to as a man; and both likings were gratified in a world of men and talk. And there was another reason too, not quite so obvious. The friendships that will go far and last long with a little impersonal dryness in them, the salt of independence, were those in which she was happy, and it was mainly with men that she found them.
>
> She felt perhaps safer with men—safer from the claims and demands of a personal relation: from some of which she shrank so instinctively that intimacy, what most people would call intimacy, was to her of the last difficulty.[5]

Her fear of intimacy is corroborated by words recorded by a friend during Wharton's final days: "I like to love, but not to [be] loved back, that is why I like so much gardens [sic]."[6] Lubbock's observations make little sense without awareness that the male company that she relished and in which she felt safe was the society of "benedicks," either confirmed bachelors such as Walter Berry or overt homosexuals such as Howard Sturgis. For the latter part of her life she surrounded herself with intellectual, verbally swift men with whom flirtation was both exciting and safe. As her niece observed, she expected ideological submission from women, but with men "she welcomed divergent points of view and adapted herself to them, feeling their stimulation."[7]

◆   ◆   ◆

The most durable and comfortable of all her male relationships was with a friend from her old New York world—the lawyer and diplomat Walter Berry. They came to know each other after her broken engagement to Harry Stevens and before her ill-fated marriage to Teddy Wharton. Apparently, she and Berry approached the idea of marrying at that time but let it pass, ostensibly because Berry had not yet established himself in a career. They were from the same social world, and she felt completely at ease with him, sharing appreciation of books, languages, and architecture. Berry was her earliest literary adviser and the first to encourage her aspirations to be a professional writer: "He helped me more than anyone, in fact he alone helped me to believe in myself."[8]

To the surprise of most of her friends, this dry, acerbic, and fastidious bachelor became the long-term companion of her life. Puzzled by Wharton's devotion to Berry, Percy Lubbock felt called upon to say that "none of her friends, to put it plainly, thought she was the better for the surrender of her fine free spirit to the control of a man . . . of strong intelligence and ability—but also, I certainly know, of a dry and narrow and supercilious temper."[9]

The primacy of this relationship is as puzzling in its way as that with Morton Fullerton. When read today by an outsider, Berry's letters to Wharton seem breezy and trivial. Flavored with words like "cheerfuller," "stummick," and "critter," they exude a raunchy, adolescent humor. On the other hand, he had considerable political importance and was a dear friend not only to Edith Wharton but to other discerning people, including Henry James and Marcel Proust.

Although for a while some assumed that Berry and Wharton were lovers, very few of her close friends really believed this.[10] Despite Berry's flirtations with women in social situations, many observers doubted that this behavior extended to a sexual interest in them. Wharton's travels with Berry suggested to Henry James and to the Berensons that they were indeed lovers, but R. W. B. Lewis treats this as a debatable question. Lewis acknowledges a "hovering and gratifying sexual element" in their long relationship but expresses doubt that Berry was greatly interested in sex with either women or men. He views Berry "as the prototype of the old-time American dandy who ogled the ladies, tugging at his moustache" and elbowing the other men knowingly.[11]

Marcel Proust's amorous letters suggest both that Berry was more substantial a person than he appeared to some observers and that he was capable of arousing powerful erotic feelings, whether or not he reciprocated them. In characteristically extravagant style, Proust praises Berry's political importance (claiming that he brought America into the war and thereby saved France), his prose style, his voice, and his physical presence. "I know of nothing more beautiful than your face or more agreeable for ears to hear than your voice. . . . I particularly hope that you realize that there is nothing at all of Monsieur de Charlus in my purely aesthetic admiration and that I speak like a collector, as if you were painted by Tintoretto." And in 1921, reminiscing about the beginning of their friendship and missing Berry's company, Proust asks himself, " 'Have I passed the age of love?' (Lafontaine, nothing of Charlus)." Frequently and excessively protesting that his love for Berry has nothing of Charlus in it, he allows, shortly before his death, that Berry is "probably the being whom I love most in the world."[12]

At times Walter Berry lived near Wharton in Paris, but as a diplomat he traveled frequently, so that their contact was often through letters and at a distance. Wharton's late reflections on this subject indicate that although she may have longed for the emotional security of marriage, she was probably more comfortable with a distanced relationship: "He wrote me a real love-letter once . . . How glad I am that I dealt with it as I did. I should never have [had] his precious friendship all my life [if] it had been otherwise."[13]

In her memoirs she wrote of him, "I suppose there is one friend in the life of each of us who seems not a separate person, however dear and beloved, but an expansion, an interpretation of one's soul. Such a friend I found in Walter Berry, [and despite separations] whenever we did meet the same deep understanding drew us together. That understanding lasted as long as my friend lived" (*Backward Glance*, 117). She concludes her tribute with: "I cannot picture what the life of the spirit would have been to me without him. He found me when my mind and soul were hungry and thirsty, and he fed them till our last hour together" (119).

Wharton's publicly expressed devotion to Berry, her desire to be buried near him, and her desolation at his death in 1927, indicate that she regarded him as her life companion. Berry was the witness of almost the whole arc of her adult life and aspirations. It was he who knew and reflected back to her the continuity of her experience. Even though he may have disappointed her in not proposing marriage after her divorce from Teddy in 1913, they faced the world in their later years very much like a couple. On the day of Walter Berry's death, she sent Gaillard Lapsley this comprehensive tribute: "All my life goes with him. He knew me all through, & wd see no one else but me" (October 12, 1927).

◆　　◆　　◆

With continuity and easy communication supplied by Berry, aesthetic conversation by Berenson, flirtation by the young men of the Queens Acre set, it was her relationship with Henry James that Wharton deemed the "pride and honor" of her life. And her life, that of an expatriate American woman fighting to realize her destiny, has been called a Henry James novel.[14] James was twenty years older than Wharton. When they started corresponding in 1900, he was at the peak of his career, she at the beginning of hers. Although the friendship began slowly, it blossomed quickly. He became her literary ideal and mentor, a source of professional counsel whom she addressed in letters as *Cher Maître*.

Their friendship was so satisfying that it supplied more mutual nurturance than many a marriage. Wharton's statement in *A Backward Glance* that "Henry James was perhaps the most intimate friend I ever had, though in many ways we were so different" (173) says a great deal about the kind of intimacy she needed. Even more than physical closeness, she desired to be registered in a sympathetic and wholly perceptive mind.

Soon he would he address her as "Beloved Edith" and "Firebird" and, in reference to her fierce energy, describe her jocularly as "the Angel of Devastation." His language reflected back to her a glorious, mythic image of herself: "Paris, as I look at it from here, figures to me a great blur of intense white light in which, attached to the hub of a revolving wheel, you are all whirled round by the finest silver strings" (April 12, 1909).[15]

Except for occasional tumultuous visits and motor trips that rather overwhelmed the aging James, the fifteen-year friendship was primarily epistolary. To both authors, letters were not a distancing of the relationship but an enhancement of it. Again and again his letters image himself as a settled barnyard fowl and Edith as a golden eagle. Her restless appetite for travel and experience overwhelmed the introspective quiet of his bachelor routines. Desiring nothing so much as to perfect his final works, he needed no new adventures. As far as outward experience goes, he had become, as one friend put it, "complete." "Be easy with me, dear Edith, be easy—my days are over for the *grande vie;* I should have been caught younger & must crawl very quietly at best through what remains to me of the *petite*" (January 31, 1909).

Protected by distance and his characteristic verbal extravagance, James could safely hint at erotic possibilities. Within tacitly understood boundaries, both could enjoy the titillation of seductive talk. They referred frequently in a language of secret innuendos to the torrid love life that George Sand had lived at Nohant with her many lovers. Once they visited together this house that they alluded to as a shrine of lustfulness. Addressing her as "My dear, dear Edith," he wrote: "I love you all the while as much as ever, & there hasn't been a day when I haven't hung about you in thought & yearned over you in spirit, & expended on you treasures of wonder & solicitude" (April 14, 1909).

Her failed marriage had left Edith Wharton deprived not only of sexual experience but of the human communication that she ardently needed. She desired above all things the sense of perfect comprehension by another human being, the sense of being fully "seen," known, and understood. In letters she could confide to James stories of her troubled marriage, love affair, and divorce and know that they were genuinely perceived. James brooded over the details in imaginative sympathy and begged for more. "But the things, the things, the things—i.e. the details—I yearn for—!" (May 9, 1909).

> I've been uncannily *haunted* in respect to your situation (that is on the side of Teddy's absence, his condition, & the conditions over there &c) with something or other in the way of an apprehension or divination of evil. . . . Please don't become unconscious of how exceedingly & intimately I am with you & how infinitely desirous of further news. (December 24, 1909)

> But my interest attaches itself to every detail. . . . my imagination & wonder play so fondly over the whole subject. . . . Well your finer appreciations will float you through *all* deep waters— & they'll become finer & finer than anything but my own appreciations *of* them! (December 30, 1909)

Henry James was the ideal spectator for a woman who needed to have her existence and her value affirmed. The quality of his attention enabled Wharton to feel cherished in the way that mattered most. In his capacious imagination she found the space in which she could extend her wings. Little wonder that he saw himself in this relationship as a hen brooding over and hatching a golden eagle.

In a sense these two shared Morton Fullerton; both wrote erotic letters to him and wrote to each other about him. It was an epistolary ménage à trois in which James abetted Wharton's sexual adventure and reveled in his imagination of their enacted love. He invited all possible details about the relationship. James dined with the two of them in their chambers at the Terminus Hotel the evening before their most celebrated night together. In 1910 he thanked her for her words about "what befell you & Morton at Chantecler. The latter circumstance intensely interests me—it floods the subject with light that in the midst of my troubles I have been *sourdement* invoking" (March 2, 1910). If Walter Berry's consciousness was the realistic mirror of Edith Wharton's selfhood, that of Henry James was the imaginative one. She required both kinds.

James functioned as her professional father and psychological mother, and she tried to ease his financial worries and agonized over the gradual failure of his health. Their concern for each other and ability to fulfill a range of emotional needs was a genuine anchor for these two souls who felt lonely amidst some of their era's best society. In this relationship both partners experienced real love and the exhilaration of an erotic dance within safe boundaries. But James, who came into Wharton's life when she needed a professional mentor, died in 1916, when she still had two decades of life ahead of her.[16]

PARENTAL INSCRIPTIONS

The Reef highlights the autobiographical forces of repression and liberation that were present in Wharton's fiction from the beginning and would continue to animate it. The figures of the repressed Anna Leath and the sexually liberated Sophy Viner symbolize dramatically elements that appear more subtly in other works of this "salamander era." Despite changes wrought by time and experience, Wharton would persist in confounding inner psychological motivations with outer societal pressures. Regardless of any drive toward social realism, she was to depict less the repressive forces of society or even the value of tradition than society as the externalized representation of her own self-imposed constraints.[17]

Much of the acceptance within the novels of this period lies within the minds of characters who, like their creator, magnify social restrictions beyond all realistic justification. Wharton's characters embrace and reinforce social conventions, utilizing them as forms of super-ego restraints. Many tales from the "salamander era" on, such as *Summer, The Age of Innocence, The Old Maid,* "The Spark," *A Son at the Front,* and *The Mother's Recompense,* inscribe variations on and splittings of Wharton's parental figures.

We observed earlier that young Edith's mother had been internalized as a punitive super-ego figure, potent far beyond her intrinsic capacity for harm, noting that much of her power had been attributed to her by the daughter's psyche. In a sense, the child magnified her mother's deficiencies into cruelty sufficient to satisfy her own need for punishment. As if to soften the complaints against her mother, Edith Wharton added that her extreme moral compunction, the "excruciating moral tortures" of her youth, were "entirely self-evolved."

This exaggerated sense of guilt must have derived from the idea that she deserved punishment for some injury to her mother—perhaps by regarding Nanny Doyley as her psychological mother, perhaps by trying to become her father's sweetheart. The denial and sacrifice of her own sexuality for so many years suggest atonement for a strong oedipal rivalry with her mother. The handsome, loving father who had aroused Edith Wharton's feminine self, who made her perceive herself as a "subject for adornment," was surely a seductive figure in her mind.

The tenderness for her father that Wharton recorded in her memoirs spills over into a preoccupation with incest that crops up with increasing frequency as her work progresses.[18] In Chapter 1 we observed that some sexually stimulating act may have occurred within the erotic environment of her father's library, where he introduced her to poetry and where she sought sexual information and had ecstatic experiences with books. We have been accumulating evidence of Wharton's sense of parental omniscience regarding sexual thoughts or acts, so that powerful male figures always know of an incipient tryst and come between a woman and her lover.

Seeking Mother, Marrying Daddy: *Summer*

Wharton's ultimate paternal interventionist is, of course, the Levantine Palmato who had coopted his daughter's sensual nature so effectively as to eliminate future competitors. If we use Wolff's date, 1919–20, for the incestuous fragment, Palmato's precursor among Wharton's published works is Lawyer Royall, the adoptive father of Charity Royall in *Summer* (1917), who not only displaces his daughter's lover but succeeds in marrying her as well. Unlike the enraptured Beatrice, this daughter tries to resist the incestuous pull, to put emotional and physical distance between herself and her father, but finds herself caught in his almost ubiquitous web. Fighting to break away but unable to formulate a realistic strategy, she becomes entrapped by her very act of separation—taking a lover and becoming pregnant. Needing to be cared for in this condition and wanting a home for her baby, she submits to marriage with her father. This joyless union represents the final defeat in her struggle for autonomy.

Charity had been informally adopted in childhood by Lawyer Royall and his wife. Following his wife's death, the lonely and somewhat seedy Royall reared the child alone. She grew up haunted by her shadowy, indeed shady, origins. She knows that she had been born of an unknown woman on The Mountain, a place thought to be inhabited by primitive folk of savage and promiscuous habits. According to Royall's story, the girl had been offered to him by her father, a man whom Royall had helped convict of manslaughter. Charity believes herself to be the child "of a drunken convict and of a mother who wasn't 'half human,' and was glad to have her go" (73). Although she was taught to be grateful to Lawyer Royall for bringing her down from the mountain and saving her from her shameful origins, she hates their constrained life in North Dormer. Seen through the eyes of this sensuous but untutored and restless adolescent, North Dormer is a trap, a place she must flee if she is to have a full life.

As Charity blossoms into lusty adolescence, neighbors who sense a potential problem in her living alone with her bachelor father urge him to send her away to school. First Royall and then Charity decline this option even though the girl feels hemmed in by the physical and cultural limitations of the town. Charity especially resents her aging surrogate father, who had propositioned her when she was seventeen (Wharton's age at her debut) and subsequently asked to marry her. She fights off her feelings of affinity to him by cultivating disgust, but her insults and rebuffs fail to destroy his possessive love for her. Wishing to earn money so that she can escape from him and from North Dormer, the scarcely literate Charity maneuvers to get herself a job as town librarian.

In the library she finds love in the form of a handsome young stranger, an architect named Lucius Harney. He represents the outer world of which this valley-bred girl has had only rare glimpses—a world of grace, manners, and culture. In the sensuous summer of her young life, Charity's love quickly flowers into passion, which Wharton renders in fiery language. Very quickly, Charity becomes pregnant, but her social inferiority makes marriage to Lucius unlikely. In her heedless and inarticulate relationship to vital forces, Charity is reminiscent of Sophy Viner, who also seizes love without asking the price or the consequences.

Lawyer Royall sniffs out the growing passion between Charity and Lucius Harney even before they themselves recognize it. Despite his fondness for Lucius, Royall is determined to intercept this love. At a high point of entrancement, when Lucius and Charity have just witnessed a thrilling display of

Fourth of July fireworks in Nettleton and hope to slip home undetected, they are spotted by Lawyer Royall, drunk and disheveled in the company of a prostitute.

> He stood staring at them, and trying to master the senile quiver of his lips; then he drew himself up with the tremulous majesty of drunkenness, and stretched out his arm.
> "You whore—you damn—bare-headed whore, you!" he enunciated slowly. (151)

Such sexual insults are designed to alienate Charity's genteel young lover, so that he will not want to marry her. They also serve to establish the girl's connections to the whole realm of primitive lusts lurking behind this father-daughter relationship. Royall's appearance in the company of a prostitute suggests that he may have had a similar connection to Charity's mother, that Charity may be his daughter, and that he regards the child of such a union as innately corrupted and therefore fair game.

Throughout the novel, Lawyer Royall's image falls between the lovers—in doorways, at moments of embrace—always he is aware of her sexual activities and contaminates them. He looms over thresholds and outside windows, haunting the girl with his unceasing vigilance. Hoping to evade this surveillance, the lovers meet secretly at a deserted cabin outside of town. There Charity is sensuously watching a fiery sunset over The Mountain and anticipating the arrival of Lucius, when she becomes "aware that a shadow had flitted across the glory-flooded room. . . . The door opened, and [in] Mr. Royall walked." He declares that he has come to prevent Charity from getting into trouble, or to help her evoke a marriage proposal from Lucius, but he concludes the episode by saying in front of Lucius that Charity is a promiscuous "woman of the town" just like her mother. "I went to save her from the kind of life her mother was leading—but I'd better have left her in the kennel she came from" (203–4).

◆   ◆   ◆

The action of *Summer* takes place within a symbolic moralized landscape. Charity is poised between the Mountain, a primitive realm of unbounded impulse (though scarcely a gratifying place), and the Town, the rigidly proper and fully encircled village of North Dormer. Charity's only knowledge of the normal world is through brief visits to the nearby town of Nettleton, a place where there are shops, circuses, even an abortionist. Had Charity been capable of escaping to Nettleton she could have moved outside the realm of extreme choices and found alternatives to both her claustrophobic world of inexorable laws and the primitive, promiscuous world of unrule. Lying outside the symbolic landscape, Nettleton represents a more flexible sort of human life, in which compromises and accommodations are possible. Like other Wharton protagonists such as Lily Bart and Newland Archer, Charity Royall seems caught between lawlessness and rigid superego demands, unable to move into the middle world of accommodation.

When we map the affective lines of force within this dreamlike novel, we find all the major characters radiating out from the central figure of Charity. Her motherless state calls forth the nurturant father in Lawyer Royall, along with his incestuous impulses. Her libido, overstimulated by having her father entirely to herself, seems to have generated The Mountain, a place of origin that would explain or justify her sense of innate pollution. Believing herself born of a degenerate mother into the morally unbounded world of The Mountain, she quite naturally accepts her instinctual nature and feels free to satisfy it. But having also been reared in prudish North Dormer, she can be persuaded that such actions are whorish.

Brought up under the Law, she is too ethical to choose abortion to solve her pregnancy crisis or to use the pregnancy to coerce Lucius into marriage. Like Sophy Viner, she is faithful to her love and refuses to corrupt it by pragmatic considerations. Torn between such polarities as the unbounded and the overly circumscribed, Charity cannot make a worldly adjustment to her situation, such as moving out of North Dormer and working to support her child. She drifts into a very bizarre solution indeed.

Charity had often felt a strange affinity to Royall, "as if she had his blood in her veins" (118). Thus Wharton deliberately inserts a hint that the adopted father may have been the biological one. By introducing this ambiguity, she fudges the incest issue, allowing readers to entertain the more piquant possibility of real incest while neutralizing it through the technicality of adoption. But either way the story is incestuous; an adoptive father is perceived as a father psychologically.

Charity's hostility toward Royall recalls Lily's toward Rosedale, a way of fending off dangerous desires. Furthermore, the author draws another line of affinity, one connecting the formerly gifted lawyer to his daughter's cultured lover, so that Lucius seems to represent Royall's spiritual son or his youthful self, the potential that has been thwarted by life in North Dormer. The relationships among characters in *Summer* are unrealistically close, all spawned by the same central imagination, which seems to have been an incestuous one.

Longing for her unknown mother begins with Charity's sexual maturation. When she first discovers her love for Lucius, she begins to yearn for her mother, no matter how disreputable this woman may turn out to be. When she finds herself pregnant and abandoned by Lucius, she fights her way through storm and weariness up to The Mountain to find her. She arrives just moments after her mother's death on a borrowed bed in a wretched hovel heated by a borrowed stove, covered in a borrowed coat. That night she sees her mother buried without even a coffin. The longed-for mother, when found, was dead, disreputable, a revolting sight—of no possible help to any daughter, much less to a pregnant one. Nonetheless, Charity had to touch the maternal base before assuming motherhood herself.

With the mother dead and Lucius engaged to someone else and unaware of her pregnancy, Charity is without resources or support. She is alone in a dangerous place, cold and hungry. Knowing all this, Royall follows her to The Mountain in a carriage, protects her from the cold, and secures food for her. He behaves tenderly enough but immediately lures her into marriage. In her shocked and vulnerable state she lacks the strength to resist him. Submitting passively, this once-fiery girl is set up to fulfill the oedipal fantasy of bringing her father a child, the child born of her youthful passion, so that her child's step-parent will be her own adoptive father. With grim fatality she surrenders for the sake of security her youth, her passion, her hopes for a fuller life. The morning after the wedding, she realizes what she has sacrificed; "for an instant the old impulse of flight swept through her; but it was only the lift of a broken wing" (280).

Social Conformity as Refuge: *The Age of Innocence*

Like *The House of Mirth*, *The Age of Innocence* is a novel of sexual inhibition that has long been read as a novel of manners. It was published in 1920, about a decade after the Fullerton affair. In it Wharton depicts a New York society of inflexible rules and rituals, an inhibitor of the instinctive life, yet a source of civilizing decencies. Like a good operatic overture, the opening scene introduces the novel's motifs, which emanate from the central question of the ambivalence of love, memorably proclaimed by Marguerite's aria, "M'ama . . . non m'ama . . . M'ama." Within Newland Archer's range of vision at this moment are representatives of his entire world—completely conventional people like the Wellands, the power networks of cousinship, social arbiters, successful challengers of the rules, arrivistes, spotless maidens, men frankly enjoying the double standard, and, above all, indicators of imminent change. The scene plunges us into a critical moment in old New York society, which was cresting just before its downward turn, a moment that is also the turning point of Archer's life.

Archer, about to end a comfortable bachelorhood in which he had never questioned the values of his class, contemplates his artfully innocent fiancée and his erotic hopes for a marriage that will miraculously reconcile "fire and ice." Almost simultaneously he receives his first impression of wider possibilities as embodied in the europeanized person of Ellen Olenska.

All this wonderfully compact exposition falls within the realm of Edith Wharton's recognized gift for social observation and satire. But the opening scene also introduces the dynamic tensions warring below the surface of this superbly constructed novel. At the same time that old New York society was defending itself against "new people," it was also yielding to innovation. Change continually challenges the stable old ways, and society manages to absorb it. Even the social arbiters who are shocked to see in the Mingott opera box a woman who has left her husband eventually invite Ellen Olenska to dinner. The illegitimate daughter of the disgraced Julius Beaufort eventually marries the Archers' son. Society's capacity for accommodation is prefigured by the quiet notation that even the gentry now find it convenient to attend the opera in public conveyances instead of private carriages. Social tolerance of individualistic behavior is best exemplified in old Catherine Mingott, daughter of a scapegrace, who loves racy conversation, lives in an unfashionable part of the city, and sleeps in a bedroom visible from the parlor—all violations of the strict code but none sufficient to diminish her social power.

Wharton's protagonists feel themselves constrained by inflexible social boundaries despite manifold examples of social change and accommodation all around them. Fundamentally conservative, Newland Archer thinks himself daring when he leaps into rash but misplaced gallantry. So exquisitely does Wharton satirize the inhibitory forces of society that we are lulled, like the characters, into accepting these forces as invincible. The inhibitory power of society is exaggerated by individuals who are afraid of their own passions.

On the verge of committing himself to what he sees as the standard destiny of a New York gentleman, Archer witnesses at the performance of *Faust* a drama of the human spirit challenging limitations, daring penalties for the privilege of enlarged experience. The legendary Faust risks damnation to look on the face of Helen. Perversely inspired by this, Newland Archer turns out to be the ultimate anti-Faust, a veritable Prufrock in disguise. He will try to break out of his limitations by reaching for what seems to be his Helen of Troy (Ellen), but he is quickly brought to heel by his own weakness and by the conjoined forces of the tribe. Indeed, the mere sight of provocative Ellen seated next to his virginal fiancée in the family opera box prompts our anti-Faust to banish temptation, to foreclose his options by announcing his engagement prematurely that very evening. His way of daring conventions (precipitate announcement, hastened wedding) serves only to put himself irreversibly within the protection of the conventions. Responsive to all that Ellen represents (vitality, sensual sophistication, "European" or bohemian values), he flies to the refuge of tradition, which he interprets as rigidly as possible. Thinking he was protecting May from contamination, he was actually protecting himself from the risks of passion.

The aria from Faust that he hears at this moment, "M'ama . . . non m'ama," speaks to Newland's doubts about marrying May Welland and to his ambivalence about committing himself to a thoroughly prescribed and predictable life. But finally, "m'ama"—he banishes these doubts by hastening to seal the marriage. However, by investing in the figure of the now-lost Ellen all that is desirable in woman, he can see May only as Ellen's opposite—invincibly virginal, even boyish, and thoroughly immune to culture.

Cherishing his image of the banished Ellen, he never allows himself to love May; he fails to bring out or develop the latent woman in her. One could think of May as a victim, a sleeping beauty whom Newland Archer declines to awaken because he is too attached to the image of her opposite. Archer is a splitter of internal images—if Ellen signifies all that is richly female and sexually desirable, May becomes to him a static icon of permanent inviolability, a Diana-figure which he visualizes as an adolescent boy. With such polarized imagery, he places desire outside the social pale and embraces renunciation. In order to retain psychic fidelity to his beloved Ellen, he renders his marriage as perfunctory, as dessicated, as possible. And when, after May's death, Newland has an opportunity to renew his relationship to Ellen, who lives a single life in Paris, he abstains even from visiting her. He cannot test his internalized Ellen against reality.

Newland's psychological conservatism is like that of Edith Wharton who, amidst all the ferment of Paris in the early twenties, chose to live in the staid Faubourg Saint-Germain and to associate, not with the people of the future such as Proust, Gertrude Stein, and Natalie Barney, but with the most conservative avatars of outmoded gentility. As Shari Benstock observes, "She dared not risk exposure to a rebellious and often risqué modernity; she needed the protection of just those social and intellectual traditions on which Proust and other moderns cast such a jaundiced eye."[19]

The aria from *Faust* addresses the paradox of marriage as Edith Wharton experienced it. For her, marriage and fidelity to the social code meant entrapment—not securing love but *foreclosing the possibility of it*. Her fiction plays endless variations on the theme of marital entrapment—enduring it, making the best of it, the social cost of evading it. Only rarely did she depict the freedom of joyfully escaping it.

Observing this conjunction of Faustian desire for unlimited experience and timid rejection of even the most available human pleasures, we marvel at the forces that bound the healthy, sensuous young Edith Wharton into a life of self-denial and, except for a brief interlude, celibacy.

Split Parental Figures: *The Old Maid*

Within an even more convention-bound version of New York society, *The Old Maid* brilliantly focuses the double-mother motif on the issue of sexual maturation. In this novella two women vie for the motherhood of Tina, a child who is biologically the daughter of one but psychologically the daughter of the other. Competition between these two mothers grows increasingly bitter as Tina approaches sexual maturity. In this compact, perfectly constructed novella, family themes and fundamental human desires are so tightly interwoven that the smallest action or intention vibrates throughout the system.

Part of Wharton's *Old New York* quartet, *The Old Maid* sharply pits conventional restraints against the rage for life. Even more uniformly than in *The Age of Innocence*, New York of the 1850s is depicted as a stifling society of "genteel monotony of which the surface was never stirred by the dumb dramas now and then enacted underground" (4). The subterranean drama of *The Old Maid* is the struggle between cousins not only for maternal rights over Tina but for possession of her as a talisman of the life force that she embodies, virtually as a genetic inheritance from her artist father.

Delia Ralston, very much a product of the stolid, conservative New York aristocracy, had renounced Clem Spender, the impecunious artist she really loved, to marry Jim Ralston, the epitome of old New York values. Clem, "tolerant, reckless, indifferent to consequences" (36), carries a surname that echoes the reference Edith Wharton once made to herself as an emotional hoarder in contrast to Morton Fullerton as an emotional spender.[20] Clem represents all the carefree emotional richness that Delia has forfeited in order to become a perfect New York matron. The pain of this loss revives when she learns that her spinsterish cousin Charlotte Lovell had once given herself to Clem and has a daughter by him: "Then for the first time Delia, with a kind of fearful exaltation, had heard the blind forces of life groping and crying underfoot" (129).

Her loss of contact with these life forces is symbolized by an ormolu clock that Clem once conveyed to her from Paris as a wedding gift from her aunt. Depicting a pastoral couple forever about to embrace, this clock is like a Grecian urn that both suspends time and marks time, reminding a woman of her youth and relentlessly tracking her distance from it. Delia keeps this clock in her bedroom because "she liked, when she woke in the morning to see the bold shepherd stealing his kiss" (17). Something of Clem's unruliness has lodged in Delia's heart and invaded the sanctity of her marriage chamber, rendering what passes there perfunctory and joyless. The clock chimes relentlessly through the story, ticking off the years that see Delia a wife, a mother, and finally a widow with Charlotte as her chief companion.

Years before, Clem Spender had consoled himself for Delia's marriage to Jim Ralston in a brief affair with her tubercular cousin Charlotte, and had then returned to Paris unaware that Charlotte was with child. Charlotte left town on the ruse of seeking a cure for her lung ailment. On her return a few years later she starts a day nursery for pauper children, among whom is one beautiful foundling named Tina, short for Clementina. Now Charlotte plans to marry Jim Ralston's equally stolid cousin Joe, assuming that she will be able to maintain contact with Tina under cover of the nursery. But Joe insists that she give up her nursery lest she contaminate any future Ralston babies by contact with the children of poverty.

Charlotte, of course, cannot part with her baby. She must cancel her wedding plans unless she can arrange to keep Tina near her. In desperation she seeks help from her cousin Delia, whom she counts on to care for Clem Spender's child, cannily sensing that Delia still cares for its father. Once Delia sees the toddler, who greatly resembles Clem, she is determined to rescue her, but at a price. She will enable Charlotte to keep her child so long as she does not bring this stigma into the Ralston family by marrying Joe. Joe's request for help in salvaging his marriage plans gives Delia her opportunity. A strategy occurs to her while she sits embroidering, holding her needle above the canvas like a "sword of Damocles":

> How easy it was, after all! A friendly welcome, a good dinner, a ripe wine, and the memory of Charlotte's eyes—so much the more expressive for all that they had looked upon. A secret envy stabbed the wife who had lacked this last enlightenment. (65)

Without consulting Charlotte and with terrible *sangfroid*, she plunges her embroidery needle into the canvas with a "sharp prick," and tells Joe that Charlotte's tuberculosis has recurred, rendering her unfit for marriage.

Delia so loves Clem's image in his daughter that she raises and eventually adopts Tina in order to keep some part of him near her. She even prefers the lively Tina to her own daughter, who, in the genetic symbolism that pervades this story, is stolid like her father. Charlotte, who lives with them after Delia becomes a widow in order to be with her child, assumes the role of spinster aunt to protect her secret. Indeed, she becomes a stereotypical "old maid," bitter, joyless, and ever vigilant that her daughter not repeat her own mistake.

On the freedom-repression axis that structures the novella, the cousins have switched poles. Charlotte, who once dared the proprieties to seize her moment of love, has rigidified and become oppressively vigilant about Tina's chastity. The formerly conventional Delia has learned how to bend social rules with impunity. She dares to adopt a child widely known to be illegitimate and later becomes indulgent toward Tina's fairly lax dating behavior. Accordingly, Tina adores Delia, calls her "Mama," and regards Charlotte as a rather grim aunt.

The adoptive relationship appears to be a great success, despite its having been shadowed by the silent struggle for mastery going on between the two mothers. The fact of Tina's developing such a blithe good nature within so poisonous an environment indicates that Wharton's attention was focused less on the daughter's psychology than on the competition between the two mothers.

Tina seems unaffected by the fact that Delia has used her to supply her own emotional deficiencies. Delia's generosity is "not for Clem Spender, hardly for Charlotte or even for Tina; but for her own sake, hers, Delia Ralston's, for the sake of her one missed vision, her forfeited reality" (130). In her identification with Tina's joyous love for the least conventional of the Halsey sons, Delia battens on Tina's youth, living out in imagination her own lost opportunities. "Never had [Delia] kept a moonlight watch with a lover's arms to warm her" (133). Throughout the wedding preparations, Delia has "been living the girl's life" in order to enjoy "that vision of requited love" (185). The woman who had been properly married to a good, solid man and borne two thriving children feels so starved for passion that she is driven to experience it vicariously through the girl whom she has appropriated emotionally.

Years before, Charlotte had counted on Delia's attachment to Clem to gain for her Tina the advantages of becoming a Ralston. The story gradually reveals that each woman has been using the other, that their close ties and shared maternity provide the insight that makes possible such intimate exploitation. The women's fine attunement to each other results from the fact that each is the other's polar opposite. Delia has had the security of marriage but has sacrificed passion, whereas Charlotte spent her emotional capital on a single relationship that offered neither continuity nor care. The reader shudders to think that after Tina's marriage Charlotte and Delia will sit facing each other for the rest of their lives, each glaring with her knowledge of the other's incompleteness.

The crucial test of true motherhood occurs on the eve of Tina's wedding, a ritual moment when mother and daughter take leave of their old relationship so that the daughter can freely enter into her new state. Which woman would share this intimate communion with the bride-to-be—the biological or the adoptive mother? Charlotte claims this moment as her inalienable right, the one event that would confirm the actuality of her motherhood. But when Delia cedes it to her and she tries to enter Tina's room, Charlotte realizes that a lifetime of emotional deprivation and bitterness has made her unfit to initiate a young girl into marriage. Delia rightly senses that Tina longs for her own "guiding hand into the new life as much as she herself yearned for the exchange of half-confidences which would be her real farewell to her adopted daughter" (175). On this issue of the mother's rights on the eve of her daughter's wedding hangs the vital question *"which of us is her mother?"* (177), an issue decided in favor of the psychological mother.

Communion between mother and daughter at this moment of passage seems more important for transmission of adult womanly capacities than for imparting sexual information. When Delia finally goes in to the expectant Tina, "they did not say much after all; or else their communion had no need of words" (189). Wharton appears to have deeply imagined every detail of this story, but especially this culminating event, as if by so doing she might rewrite her own wedding eve into a maternal blessing. If so, in awarding the preference to the psychological mother, the author imaginatively drives a knife into the heart of the biological mother.

THE ARTISTIC HERITAGE

Clem Spender shares artistic traits with a series of male characters drawn from Wharton's own paternal imagery. The architect Lucius Harney of *Summer* sketches houses and cherishes books, Mason Grew ("His Father's Son") loves music and language, John Campton is a painter, Hayley Delane ("The Spark") once cared for poetry, like Lily Bart's father and many other Wharton men. Perhaps the best known of Wharton's shy poetic men is Newland Archer of *The Age of Innocence*, and the most appealing may be Ralph Marvell of *The Custom of the Country*. Whether their aesthetic interests are dominant or vestigial, in most cases these men are married to worldly women who value financial over intellectual assets. This recurring pattern seems to stem from Wharton's grief for her own father's wasted potential, a loss that she attributed to her mother.

Eventually, however, she tried shifting away from the wife the onus for a man's failure to realize his potential. She came to realize that if men choose frivolous wives and permit the erosion of their talents, perhaps, like Hayley Delane and

Newland Archer, they find other ways of channeling their gifts. Or perhaps these gifts are minor.

In such stories as "His Father's Son" and "The Spark," Wharton probes yet more deeply into the issue of wasted talent. In "The Spark," a young male narrator investigates the hidden spark of Hayley Delane, an older man married to a flirtatious and contemptuous wife. To the young man, Delane is a person of consequence even though he appears to be a typical New York aristocrat—interested in polo, poker, hunting. Delane had once read the standard poets but now shows no interest in literature and even regards as rubbish the poetry of Walt Whitman, whom he had known as a military nurse during the Civil War. Marveling that it was not Hayley but the wife who "ruled and he who bent the neck," the narrator wonders whether she had trivialized Delane but eventually divines that something deeper had caused loss of the spark.

Finally, he could not blame Delane's loss of bookishness on the wife—perhaps he had just stopped developing around the age of nineteen, near the end of the Civil War, which he had felt more strongly than the rest of his generation:

> Little sympathy as I felt for Mrs. Delane, I could not believe it was his marriage which had checked Delane's interest in books. . . . I found, for several layers under the Leila stratum, no trace of any interest in letters; and I concluded that, like other men I knew, his mind had been receptive up to a certain age, and had then snapped shut on what it possessed, like a replete crustacean never reached by another high tide. (54–55)

Delane seems to have derived his moral development from the example of Walt Whitman's nurturing behavior while caring for Civil War wounded. To Whitman's internalized example Delane owes his only "original" or socially aberrant behavior, which is taking care of his wife's outcast disreputable father. The narrator's quest into the mystery of Delane's personality reveals a split between two kinds of specialness or "spark"—moral or nurturing instincts, as distinguished from susceptibility to literature. In this remarkable novella Wharton dissects the paternal figure and separates the nurturing father from the artistic one. She is on her way to looking outside the biological father for the source of her own artistry.

The issue was of great personal moment because Wharton never quite relinquished the notion that artistic gifts are inherited from the paternal side. If her father's poetic leanings were minor, perhaps he was not the father of her talent. And there is reason to believe that she at least fantasized that a more gifted man was really her father. Her creative passion, both a gift and a problem for her, was bound up with her sexuality, perhaps giving her multiple reasons for speculating that her biological father may not have been the kindly and handsome George Frederic Jones but someone "extremely cultivated," such as her brothers' English tutor.

Perhaps this is an artist's version of the family romance— an alternate father imagined to be the source of one's genius. Had the tutor been her father, as most probably he was not, there would have been the added advantage of making the very attractive Mr. Jones no longer her father and therefore no longer forbidden by the incest taboo. Wharton's experience of a divided mother, that is, an unloving mother and a loving nanny, could have suggested the notion of a father divided between the biological and the sustaining functions. In any case, rumors about Wharton's paternity abounded during her lifetime. According to the detailed account given by R. W. B. Lewis, she did nothing to squelch these rumors and even encouraged them.[21] Possibly, in a playful spirit, she may even have started them. In any case, she did let her imagination elaborate them in both *Age of Innocence* and "His Father's Son."

M. Rivière, the lively, cultivated, and conversation-loving French tutor in *The Age of Innocence,* is set up in contrast to people in the laconic social world of Newland Archer. Newland is drawn to him as the embodiment of all that he thinks New York society lacks, but his conventional and class-conscious wife discourages the friendship. Wharton endows Rivière with the traits of an ideal father for her talent, all that

Wharton herself found lacking in American life. She even teases us with the possibility that Rivière might once have been the lover of Countess Olenska and enlarges Rivière's place in the novel to the extent that it becomes obtrusive, a noticeable flaw in the novel's economy.

The imaginative splitting of her own father along the lines of "real" versus "adoptive" is played out ingeniously in *A Son at the Front*. This book seriously explores the nature of parenting, essentially splitting or doubling both parental figures to examine the respective contributions of both the biological and the surrogate parents to the personality of a son. Most pointedly, it examines the formation of the son's aesthetic sensibilities by dividing the paternal functions between a father and a step-father, thus distinguishing nature from nurture.

Young George Campton derives his innate sensitivity to the arts from his painter-father, John Campton, but the specific character of his aesthetic interests is shaped by his exposure to the fine library of his step-father, a wealthy banker named Anderson Brant. Brant is married to George's mother Julia, a vain and worldly woman who had divorced Campton because of infidelity and generally irregular behavior. Brant is so devoted to his step-son that Campton finally comes to consider him George's "dry nurse," a necessary provider of sustenance and stability. With the paternal functions thus divided, the action centers on the question of which is the real father, much as *The Old Maid* asks which is the real mother.

Receptivity to the arts is traced to the separate streams of biology and cultivation. From exposure to his step-father's rare-book collection, young George reads "as only a book-worm reads—reading with his very finger-tips, and his inquisitive nose, and the perpetual dart ahead of a gaze that seemed to guess each phrase from its last word" (29). The boy is destined to be an appreciator of art rather than an artist; he plans to follow Brant in becoming a banker when he returns from war, but a banker who treasures books. Both fathers vie for their share of George, with the banker coming off somewhat better than the artist.

In the course of their necessary dealings with each other, the two fathers confront and eventually work out the conflicts generated by their love for the same son. Brant is so generous and thoughtful that usually he outdoes the more egotistical Campton, who grumbles: "Was it always to be Brant who thought first of the things to make George happy—always Brant who would alone have the power to carry them out?" (378). Understandably jealous, Campton finds that "between himself and his son he seemed to see Mr. Brant's small suffering profile" (381), and, despite efforts at self-control, he resents it.

The artist with unreliable income cultivates contempt for the banker's millions:

> "Do you suppose I'd have wasted all these precious years [painting portraits] if I hadn't wanted to make my son independent of you? And he *would* have been, if the war hadn't come; been my own son again and nobody else's, leading his own life . . . instead of having to waste his youth in your bank, learning how to multiply your millions." (251–52)

But when George is wounded during the war, the two fathers go to the front together to visit their son. Although deeply pained himself, Brant shows great delicacy in ceding priority to Campton. Anderson Brant's decency and sensitivity finally erode Campton's hostility; they learn to share what remains of the dying boy and eventually to share his memory. At a difficult time "Mr. Brant was the only person with whom, at this particular juncture, [Campton] cared to talk of George" (347).

The two men bond so firmly as to exclude George's self-centered mother. Campton wonders how such an empty, frivolous woman would deal with the loss of her son: "If Julia discovered, as she could hardly fail to do, how much more deeply Brant had loved her son than she had, and how much more inconsolably he mourned him, that would only increase her sense of isolation" (422). Motherhood rarely suffers so great a slap as Wharton delivers here. Julia Campton Brant is not only less parental than George's father, she is less caring than his step-father. In the circle of family love, she is trivial and irrelevant.

ROLE REVERSAL: *THE MOTHER'S RECOMPENSE*

In 1925, at age sixty-three, Wharton published a singularly acrobatic variant of her mother-daughter theme, one in which the roles are reversed, so that the daughter becomes the nurturer of the mother. In *The Mother's Recompense*, Kate Clephane, a middle aged "prodigal mother"[22] who had abandoned her husband and young daughter for free love and a roving life in Europe, returns to New York to resume her role as mother to her now-grown daughter, Anne. Socially, the divorced woman has lived as a displaced person, passing her time among other rootless people at the less expensive European watering spots. The daughter, on the other hand, is securely positioned in New York society, in the world and life that Kate has forfeited for freedom.

When the book opens, Kate awakens in her room on the Riviera to receive a telegram that she hopes is from the young lover who left her some years before. Instead it is from Anne, declaring that Mrs. Clephane, Kate's former mother-in-law, has died. It is followed by a second message inviting Kate to return to America. Quickly she abandons her youthful garments and buys a sedate wardrobe in which to resume her abandoned position as mother and New York matron. She is received warmly and graciously by Anne, now owner of the house over which Kate had once presided. With Anne's skillful management of the awkward situation, the two get on famously.

Reveling in Anne's exquisite solicitude, Kate is ready to abandon her rootless way of life and take up her part in the starchy world she had once escaped. She yearns to attain and preserve a symbiotic mother-daughter relationship, but with the roles reversed, so that she is the cosseted object of her nurturing daughter's care. Seeing that Anne is of marriageable age, she worries that someone may break into their new-found intimacy. She scans the social scene to detect and intercept suitors and tries to minimize the influence of loose women in Anne's social set. Within a year her worst fears are fulfilled; Anne does fall in love—and with her mother's former lover, Chris Fenno.

Not a little like Morton Fullerton, Fenno is so talented a lover that women can forgive him anything. Despite his neglect, Kate has never stopped hoping for a resumption of their affair. He is casual, pleasure-seeking, artistic, and morally "careless." He claims not to have known when he met Anne that she was the daughter of Kate Clephane, but we suspect that a slightly incestuous attachment to a very rich and gifted young woman would not have disturbed him unduly.

Regarding the engagement as an abomination, an "incestuous horror," Kate tries desperately, but in the end unsuccessfully, to terminate it. Like her mother, Anne insists on her sexual rights. Finally, Kate has to undergo the torture of giving away the bride at Anne's wedding to Chris. To avoid the discomfort of living next door to this young couple, Kate comes close to marrying her old friend, Fred Landers. But impulsively she boards the next steamer to France and resumes her old life on the Riviera with her one constant companion, her maid Aline. With Anne's marriage, Kate seems to yield the field to her daughter, turning over the sexual role to the next generation.

Wharton indicated to a friend that the book's epigraph from Shelley, "Desolation is a delicate thing," was the key to its meaning. The book ends with renunciation but hardly with desolation. Kate has renounced life with her daughter under conditions that seem to her abominable, and not unreasonably so. In an act that troubles most readers, she also renounces marriage to the faithful family friend who offers the security she craves, in favor of an epistolary relationship with him. Her assertion that his weekly letters are the blessing of her exiled existence seems closer to the psychology of Edith Wharton than to that of Kate Clephane.

Perhaps the epigraph is a sly allusion to Shelley's statement that incest is very poetical, the idea on which he based "The Cenci." A portrait of Beatrice Cenci appears in the Clephane house, as it does in many Wharton settings. As we have seen, oblique incest, that is, incest at one remove from technical actuality, runs through Wharton literature. In *The Mother's Recompense* the incest theme is interwoven with Kate's satisfaction in being nurtured by her own child, so that generational strife over the same lover intercepts the satisfaction of an infantile need on the part of the mother.

Outside the Kate-Anne axis, a sort of super-mother in the form of Kate's mother-in-law, governs the actions. The mother-in-law's disapproval had soured Kate's marriage and her severe strictures had kept Kate away from Anne all those years. Only after the senior Mrs. Clephane's death does Anne dare invite her mother to return. This formidable dowager who stood between Kate and the fulfillment of her maternal identity hovers over the novel as she had hovered over the life of her daughter-in-law, as a major repressive force.

A child's point of view seems to invoke the book's repeated references to the mother-in-law's face. A child tends to read its own value from the most expressive features of its mother's face, the brows and lips. We see "the forbidding line of old Mrs. Clephane's lips" (66) and "her obstinate brows" (68), the latter inherited by Anne, who has her own kind of obstinacy. The hovering maternal scorn of Mrs. Clephane's face is subtly opposed to the infantile desires of Kate Clephane—for nurturance, for sensory satisfaction, and for secure possession of the maternal object. What Kate really yearns for in middle age, then, is not a lover, a husband, or a stable social position, but perfect nurturance by an idealized mother who will be secured to her by the bond of blood. Because this early deficit cannot be compensated by anyone, not by a husband and certainly not by a married daughter, Kate opts for the salaried attendance of her servant Aline.

Invariably in Wharton's fiction, mothers-in-law freeze their sons' wives with scowling disapproval. They find their daugh-

ters-in-law insufficiently attentive to their marital duties and
all too ready to deviate from tradition, as in the frequently
repeated motif of brides resetting the family jewels. These
powerful women carry some of the charge remaining from
Edith Wharton's humiliating subjection to the disapproval of
Mrs. Paran Stevens, the society matron who declined to be
Edith's mother-in-law by breaking up her engagement to her
son Harry. Although Harry Stevens (who died shortly afterward) seems to have left little lasting impress on Edith, his
mother's rejection remained a bitter potion for life. Her dis-
missal seems to have resonated with all the maternal rejection
that Edith carried over from childhood and served as an accept-
able lightning rod for her feelings.[23]

Told from the viewpoint of one who has been unwomaned
by maternal rejection, *The Mother's Recompense* might well
have been called "the mother's renunciation." Twice Kate renounces motherhood—first in leaving her child to go off with
a lover, second in leaving America after Anne's marriage. Unable to be wife or mother or even for very long a lover, Kate
Clephane walks out on Anne and her New York world in favor
of an unanchored life in southern France with a trusted
woman servant. The serving woman Aline, whose name recalls that of Wharton's housekeeper Elise, seems to be the best
recompense available to a woman who was never comfortable
with family relationships.[24]

5

Final Adjustments

"You have to go plumb down to the Mothers to fish up
the real thing."
                        Vance Weston in *The Gods Arrive*

In her final decade Edith Wharton was remarkably productive; she produced a massive volume of work that includes
some of her best short fiction. At the age of sixty-six, although
disheartened and ill, she completed a best-selling novel (*The
Children*) and began the first of several long works, including
three novels and a memoir. In 1928, the year of Teddy Wharton's death in New York and the year following Walter Berry's
death in Paris, she started work on her chaotic two-volume
artist story, *Hudson River Bracketed* and *The Gods Arrive*. The
major works of her final period move from the specious serenity of her memoir to the genuine serenity of *The Buccaneers*,
her last novel. In the memoir she presented herself through a
magisterial persona, that of a *grande dame* reviewing her well
organized and purposeful life. The autobiographical mode
had lured her into a flattering self-portrait. To confront her
existential realities, she required the distancing of fiction.

The transformational work running through her life and
career needed revision to meet the emotional demands of old
age. The writings of her last decade were shaped by these exigencies; they enabled her to connect the course of her life to her
present and future needs. They helped give meaning to her life
as she prepared for death. They served as a life review reorga-
nizing her past and as a valorization of herself as a woman of

letters—no small triumph for a writer with lifelong gender problems. The very last novel, although left uncompleted, brings an adolescent girl very much like the young Edith Wharton into society, love, and marriage through the guidance of an auxiliary mother in the form of an ideal governess.

The two Vance Weston novels, *Hudson River Bracketed* and *The Gods Arrive*, form a single quest story, a genre in which privation, error, and struggle serve as preparation for ultimate greatness. Through the quest theme of this kunstlerroman even Wharton's childhood deprivations and adult losses acquired purpose. As her artist-character, Vance Weston, concluded after reviewing his struggles, "those hours had been the needful prelude to whatever he had accomplished since. 'You have to go plumb down to the Mothers to fish up the real thing' " (*Gods*, 118). By writing her way through Weston's quest, Wharton would transform her early deprivations into the preconditions of her own artistic triumph. By setting primal Mothers as the goal of Weston's quest, Wharton found a way to link her own identity themes to larger mythic ones. This distancing enabled her to convert the rejecting mother of her childhood into the maternal image she needed to conclude her life peacefully.

In the massive bildungsroman of Vance Weston she worked through to yet another version of the mother theme. She was able to tell her own story more truthfully by telling it disguised and slant, as someone else's story, as a man's story. For most of her life, Wharton had envisioned her creative self as masculine and her artists as almost invariably male. Vance Weston's tortured quest for the Mothers gives an important new twist to the self-story Wharton had been telling at earlier stages of her life; it revises the gender imagery of creative origins. As she moves the scene of artistic genesis from a father's library to a woman's library and gives woman a generative role in the formation of an artist (albeit a male one), Wharton moves closer to unifying her feminine self and her artistic self. But first she has to transform the negative memory of her actual mother into a more generalized mythic image of the eternal feminine, a mother image good enough to be the foundation of her artistic self.

By this time she realized that when her life closed, only her books would remain for posterity. Leaving behind no fleshly children, she needed to regard the library and all that it symbolized as her own legitimate realm, the realm of a woman of letters. Her longstanding quest to unify her feminine and her creative selves would now be approached through goddess myths. Myths of the earth mother or mother goddess were being revived in Wharton's time; they would have been accessible to her through her beloved Goethe, through Johann Bachofen's *Das Mutterrecht* (1861), and through their appearance in American fiction by Hemingway, Faulkner, and Cather.[1]

The subject was in the air, but Wharton was drawn to it not by intellectual fashion but by the urgent personal needs of the penultimate stage of her life. She had repeatedly tried to reconstruct her inner mother, not only to repair damage to this image but to adapt it to the requirements of successive phases of her life. Fiction helped her imagine ways of doing this. We have traced this process in such works as "The Touchstone," *The House of Mirth, Summer,* and *The Old Maid.* The final works constitute a distinct phase in her effort to create for herself the mother of her deepest needs. Although she seems to have approached a vision of such mothering in *The Buccaneers,* her ability to rely on it to the end is problematical.

THE MAKINGS OF AN ARTIST: *HUDSON RIVER BRACKETED* AND *THE GODS ARRIVE*

Hudson River Bracketed, the novel completed in 1929, had been started in 1913 as "Literature," a story set in the years and locales of Wharton's youth. Its many autobiographical details include a nursemaid called by Doyley's first name, Hannah.[2] In both volumes of the Vance Weston novel, Wharton distributed aspects of herself among various characters—Vance Weston, Emily Lorburn, and Halo Tarrant—none superficially recognizable as a self-representation.[3] More identifiable are figures who had played important roles in her life—husband Teddy Wharton, lover Morton Fullerton, lifelong friend and mentor Walter Berry (touchingly portrayed as the faithful witness of Halo Tarrant's life, Frenside, or "a friend at one's side"). This distribution of herself and major figures of her life into fictive characters allowed her to set aspects of her own life experience into dramatic interaction, to discover fresh new patterns in the old materials.

Through the sequence of Vance Weston's literary works she reveals various ways in which artists represent their lives in fiction, moving from virtually direct expression of personal pain, through various kinds of displacements and indirection, and on to mythic transformations. In tracing Vance Weston's fictive transformations of his own tumultuous trajectory in time, space, and human relationships, Wharton charted the links between her own life experiences and her artistic imagination.

Like Wharton, Vance has a mother who might have been good enough for a less sensitive person but who fails to meet an artist's very special requirements. Wharton implies that the reactivity of the creative spirit intensifies needs and hungers, magnifies deficiencies. Even Vance's secondary nurturing figure, Grandma Scrimser, a woman congenial to his spiritual needs, does not suffice. Weston still has to seek through great travail a mother adequate to the demands of his creativity. Finding fragments of such a figure in his various lovers—pliant admiration in Laura Lou, intellectual camaraderie and self-sacrifice in Halo Tarrant, sheer sensuality in Floss Delaney, Weston pursues women in search of the one who might embody all of these. He seeks for one woman who can be his muse, his lover, and the mother of his child. Vance needs long preparation before he can recognize all of this in Halo. The novels further suggest that the mother adequate for an artist is not merely found in the external world but is *created* by the artist through suffering and active self-preparation. In other words, grounding himself as a creator is Vance's fundamental act of creation.

Oddly enough, Vance Weston, an unformed youth from the provinces, all appetite but lacking in culture and discipline, serves to represent aspects of the highly cultivated but self-educated Edith Wharton. His intellectual development and literary career follow the pattern of Wharton's. Before coming East, Vance was, like Wharton, hungry for knowledge, for a usable cultural heritage. As Wharton, who received no formal schooling, said of herself,

> I have often sighed, in looking back at my childhood, to think how pitiful a provision was made for the life of the imagination behind those uniform brownstone facades, and have concluded that since, for reasons which escape us, the creative mind thrives best on a reduced diet, I probably had the fare best suited to me. ("A Little Girl's New York," 357)

Wharton had educated herself in her father's library—learning literature, philosophy, and religion with hungry passion. With similar voracity, Vance Weston discovers literature in Emily Lorburn's library. This library has been kept intact as a shrine to the deceased Miss Lorburn; it is dominated by her relics and a commanding portrait of her reading a book. Vance starts his literary education with the volume Miss Lorburn had been reading when she died, Coleridge's "Kubla Khan," and moves on to a discovery of literature under the tutelage of the dead woman's niece, Halo Tarrant. He spends months working his way through Miss Lorburn's books, coming to feel a deep rapport with the creator of the Willows and its library.

For Vance Weston this whole cluster of experiences—Miss Lorburn, her library, and her home—"symbolized continuity, that great nutritive element of which no one had ever told him, of which neither Art nor Nature had been able to speak to him, since nothing in his training had prepared him for their teaching. Yet, blind puppy, groping embryo as he was, he had plunged instantly into that underlying deep when the Willows had given him a glimpse of it" (498).

The Lorburn library is the starting point of Weston's quest

and is to be its culmination. Between the beginning and the end of his journey lies a period of compulsive change—a continual decamping from every place, person, or circumstance. As soon as he attains what he seeks, he discovers new desires. Weston's restlessness is an intensified version of Edith Wharton's tendency to buy and decorate new homes, take off on impulsive journeys, keep in motion. Author and character share an insatiable drive for the right kind of knowledge, the right place to be in the world, a home for the body that is also a home for the spirit. Eventually, Edith Wharton divided herself between two homes in France, each with its own library.

Wharton endowed Weston with her own cognitive style and temperament—marked mood swings, hyperreactivity, restlessness, and hunger for experience. Of herself she said, "I was like Egmont's Clärchen, 'now wildly exultant, now deeply downcast,' and always tossed on the waves of a passionate inner life. I never felt anything *calmly*—and I never have to this day!" ("Life and I," 41). This extreme responsiveness caused a fear of being overwhelmed by intense experiences, leading her to limit exposure to them and to live, as she said, "on a reduced diet," letting her imagination supply the richness. "Snatches, glimpses—the seeds of things—that's what story-tellers want," says Vance Weston (*Gods*, 18).

> [Vance] realized that, instead of seizing the opportunity to explore every nook of [the house], he had sat all the afternoon in one room, and merely dreamed of what he might have seen in the others. But that was always his way: the least little fragment of fact was enough for him to transform into a palace of dreams, whereas if he tried to grasp more of it at a time it remained on his hands as so much unusable reality. (*Hudson*, 71)

Similarly, Vance becomes so overexcited by the beauty of a Gothic cathedral that he wants "to push back the overwhelming spectacle till he had the strength to receive it. . . . When the impressions were too abundant and powerful they benumbed him" (*Gods*, 22, 37).

Both character and author are driven people who cannot settle for ordinary satisfactions. They seek experiences that will appease their hunger for meaning, and bring all of life under the control of a dominant idea. They try to place themselves at the pole or axis of life from which significance derives. For both, life is an existential journey from some kind of original deprivation into a career that they hope will unite all the urges, drives, and ambitions into a central religious quest. For both of them, creativity has a sexual origin and a religious goal.

In "Life and I" Wharton intimated that her passionate attachment to the written word had a sexual genesis—that libraries, books, and the act of narration had become libidinized for her. A similar nexus is reflected in the fact that Weston's first story, "One Day," is written as a reaction to the sexual insult of his grandfather's seduction of Vance's first girlfriend, Floss Delaney. This quasi-incestuous episode initiates a suicidal depression that Vance eventually masters by means of the written word:

> He began hastily, feverishly, the words rushing from his pen like water from a long-obstructed spring, and as the paragraphs grew it seemed to him that at last he had found out a way of reconciling his soul to its experiences. He would set them down just as they had befallen him in all their cruel veracity, but as if he were relating the tragedy of somebody else. (*Hudson*, 32)

Only gradually does he learn that the scarcely modified personal experience of what he calls his "me-book" is too subjective, that "if he goes on retailing the successive chapters of his own history, as they happen to him, they'll be raw autobiography, or essays disguised as novels" (231–32). The course of his authorial career is a search for a workable relationship between lived experience and art. Throughout his experimentations, he is always certain that the origin of his "furor scribendi" was the sexual insult of witnessing his grandfather's seduction of his own first love.

Vance Weston's fictionalization of experience goes through many stages. His magnum opus, *Colossus*, attempts to graduate from breadth of experience to depth, from the personally unique to the mythicized universal. Intended to be his climactic achievement, this book turns out to be too personal, too ambitious, and too amorphous to be an artistic success, but writing it leads him toward personal salvation.

Hudson River Bracketed and *The Gods Arrive* take Weston through a lifetime of sensual indulgence and restless change seeking contact with the chthonic Mothers of the Faust legend, who he hopes will anchor his fiction in the depths of experience. Vance is haunted by the scene in which Faust "descends to the Mothers." Faust "must have wound round and round like this," he thinks.

> Vance thought of the Cretan labyrinth, of Odysseus evoking the mighty dead, of all the subterranean mysteries on whose outer crust man loves and fights and dies. The blood was beating in his ears. He began to wish they might never find the right door, but go on turning about forever at the dark heart of things. (*Gods*, 23)

The way to the primal source is indirect, found only by wandering and suffering. Implicitly, the story justifies Vance's sexual infidelities as a quest for *die Ewige Weibliche*, the Eternal Feminine. The sensory hungers of the artist, his almost tropic drive toward the Mothers, is treated not as libertinism but as the condition of his genius.

In certain ways Vance Weston's sexual career, his bisexuality and his dalliances with a long series of women, reflects that of Edith Wharton's lover, Morton Fullerton. Wharton used the Weston books to derive still newer meanings from that old relationship. Like Halo Tarrant, Wharton was somewhat older than her lover, more experienced in the literary world, and maternal in her relationship to him. Halo exhibits the noble attitude Wharton had tried to take toward Fullerton—that of total submission to her lover and his putative genius, as one who asks nothing for herself but the opportunity to serve him. As passion subsided and the men began to feel stifled by such high-minded self-abnegation, both women tried to salvage the relationship by becoming good comrades. During her own love affair Wharton acknowledged Fullerton's right to move on to other women and grumbled only about his bad faith in deceiving her. As she came to understand the role of the erotic in human life and especially in the sensibilities of artists, she came to see free-floating sensuality as a concomitant of the artist's special gifts.

She also found new and subtler uses for the maternal role in love. She realized that it should not be limitless, one-sided self-sacrifice. Halo had to learn, as Wharton once did, that masochistic subservience was not the way to hold her lover or even to serve him well. She must develop self-sufficiency and respect her own form of generativity rather than to live through his. Halo comes to see the egotism lurking under exaggerated female submission and learns to insist on mutuality in love.

After eight hundred pages of affairs with various types of women in various kinds of relationship, Vance Weston makes contact with the long-sought Mothers when he returns to the Willows and embraces his estranged Halo. Feeling like a weary and disgraced child, he comes to rest finally in the arms of his pregnant former mistress. Halo has become the Magna Mater of Goethe's *Faust*, a mother figure that includes the sanctified sinner Gretchen. As Vance Weston's muse, Halo becomes the mother of his genius as well as the mother of his child. She will make a home for Vance's restive spirit in the former house of Emily Lorburn, the presiding spirit of the library.

His pilgrimage to the maternal fount of his creativity concludes in the kind of resolution that Wharton was seeking for herself—finding a way to derive essential nurturance by moving beyond the biological mother (with her inevitable faults) to the ideal maternal principle that each of us carries within. For author and character, life is an odyssey that brings the seeker back to the original home, having learned through painful experience how to derive sustenance from it.

To become a good mother, either biologically or generatively, one must have had a mother. And Edith Wharton needed not only to *have* had a mother, but to feel that she still in some way had one to see her through the helplessness of old age. In her last years she needed also to feel that in the larger sense of contributing to the future of the race, she, too, was a mother. She entered the maternal lineage by imagining for herself a generative role. The self Wharton had achieved over a lifetime as a woman of letters, becomes, in the fictive figure of Emily Lorburn, the mythic primal mother Weston had been seeking. Halo is his guide to her.

In the course of her life, Edith Wharton had moved from her biological mother to a surrogate mother, to internalized images of nurturant figures, and finally to a mythicized maternal principle. Through this process she found a way to include herself in the matriarchal chain—to move from a needy daughter to a self-educated woman, to a writer, to a generative force in the world of affairs. To consolidate this progression, she imaged herself as Emily Lorburn, the presiding genius and proprietor of the kind of book collection she had grown up thinking of as a "gentleman's library."

Perhaps Wharton's greatest creative act was the forging through her own intellect and imagination what life had denied her—an inner mother that would suffice. Having done so, she could, entirely without children, place herself in the matriarchal line. With certain aspects of her experience channeled into Vance Weston and others into the mother figures Emily Lorburn and Halo Tarrant, Wharton created for herself a new role—simultaneously as the needy artist and as the Mothers he required to guide him to creative maturity. In becoming mother to this artist, Wharton symbolizes the process of generating and authorizing a viable self, in this case the creative self. In seeing herself as both the artist in need of a maternal progenitor and also as that female progenitor,

Edith Wharton provided herself with a symbolic mother, or, to feminize Erik Erikson's famous concept, became her own mother.

Reflexively, Weston repaid the benefit by imagining and recreating the life of his progenitor, the author in the guise of Emily Lorburn. With Halo providing encouragement and factual background, he recreates Emily Lorburn as Alida, the heroine of his own historical novel, called *Instead*. He imaginatively reconstructs Miss Lorburn's obliterated past and in doing so intuits that she had experienced a secret life. At first he had accepted her spinsterly reputation and pitied her lack of sexual experience: "Poor Emily—I supposed she dreamed of a Lohengrin . . . and hoped to find a baby in the bulrushes. . . . And she ended in spectacles, cold and immaculate, reading Coleridge all alone" (*Hudson*, 133). But musing in Miss Emily's library he perceives intuitively that she was "sad but not shrunken . . . her long thin hands full of gifts for some one. . . . Instead of withering she had ripened. Her books, and some inner source of life, had kept her warm;—he wondered how? And suddenly a queer idea came to him" (333)—Miss Emily had known love. How slyly Wharton insinuates her own history of rejuvenation through a secret experience of passion!

Having served as Weston's inspiration, the *genius loci* of the Willows and its library is inscribed into a book, and thereby enters into the generative chain of literature. By the end of *The Gods Arrive*, Miss Emily's niece Halo receives a matured Vance at the Willows and announces that she carries his child. Through her niece, Miss Emily thus enters into the biological chain as well. And Vance Weston, by joining himself to the Lorburn maternal heritage through his prospective child, becomes a link in a chain extending from the past into the future.

The Weston books are far from masterpieces, but they served life purposes for their author and made possible a better novel, *The Buccaneers*, which brought up from the depths memories of both of Edith Wharton's mothers, her biological mother and her psychological one, the beloved Doyley.

DOYLEY REDUX: *THE BUCCANEERS*

With *The Buccaneers*, an unfinished and posthumously published novel,[4] Wharton recovers her light satiric touch and
graceful style. Here, at the very end of her life and career, she
confronts a version of her own "double mother" theme but
advances it in time from the mother-nanny dichotomy of
childhood to a mother-governess one of late adolescence. By
this means, the auxiliary mother moves forward in the life
course to help a young woman meet the sexual needs of young
adulthood. In *The Buccaneers* a governess enters the life of
Nan St. George when she is sixteen, a time of transition to the
adult world of marriage and society. Nan's mother, needing
social guidance, has retained a governess to "finish" her brilliant, artistic, but not quite pretty younger daughter, Annabel
St. George, known as Nan.

Like her creator, Nan hungers for beauty, for rich experience, for a life that meets the needs of her imagination. Endowed with Wharton's own highly reactive temperament, the
kind that would make adjustment to conventional life difficult, the essentially anarchic Nan needs a very specific kind of
mother. Sharing Wharton's volatility, her tendency toward
extremes of feeling, Nan needs an emotional environment
that can contain her without imprisoning her.

Unlike Nan's flaccid mother, the governess has just the
right traits. Laura Testvalley is "an adventuress, but a great-
souled one" (357). She knows when to give in and when to
hold the line, is intuitive about a young girl's feelings and
ready with comfort and understanding. Her "astringent" style
of sympathy sustains the girl without encouraging self-pity;
"though Miss Testvalley was often kind, she was seldom tender" (335). These specific traits reflect Edith Wharton's dis-
taste for sentimentality and preference for intellectual and
personal toughness.

Although cannily prudent about the property basis of society, Laura Testvalley knows when to subordinate such concerns to love and personal fulfillment. She has had a complete

worldly education and can deal comfortably with sexuality in its many forms, whether it be casual, extramarital, or church-sanctified. Wharton supplies her with an Italian background and reinforces the significance of that Latin imagery by giving Brazil an oddly prominent role in the story. Any form of contact with Brazil seems to unravel Anglo-Saxon inhibitions and liberate the instincts. The experience of working on a Brazilian plantation loosens up the social behavior of several of the young men. The most unashamedly sensuous of the "buccaneering" girls, Conchita de Santos-Dios (but known by her step-father's name, Closson) comes from Brazil. Wharton perhaps borrows Thomas Mann's way of symbolizing sensuality and artistry by deriving it from "swifter, more perceptive" Latin blood. Laura Testvalley, a cousin to Dante Gabriel Rossetti, easily shrugged off her youthful sexual encounter with Lord Richard:

> The Lord Richard chapter was a closed one, and she had no wish to re-open it. She had paid its cost in some brief fears and joys, and one night of agonizing tears; but perhaps her Italian blood had saved her from ever, then or after, regarding it as a moral issue. In her busy life there was no room for dead love-affairs. (75)

She is later capable of trading on this old connection to get an invitation to the Assembly Ball for the girls she is trying to launch socially.

Laura Testvalley, with her knowledge of the world and appreciation of the needs of such a volatile girl as Nan, becomes the psychological mother. When lonely and disappointed, Nan would curl up in bed with Laura and ask her to read poetry to her, sometimes even falling asleep there. One evening Laura reads Rossetti's "The Blessed Damozel" to Nan. They talk of love and romance until Nan drifts into slumber. "Miss Testvalley murmured on, ever more softly, to the end; then blowing out the candle, she slid down to Nan's side so gently that the sleeper did not move. 'She might have been my own daughter,' the governess thought, composing her narrow frame to rest, and listening in the darkness to Nan's peaceful breathing" (90).

Fulfilling the fantasy of many a nanny-reared child, Nan becomes her governess's favorite. In this special instance, a genuine filial bond is established that will eventually stand up to the ultimate tests—that Laura should sacrifice her own interests for Nan's and will return when needed even though, like every nanny or governess, she will have moved on to the care of other young ladies. Like an ideal mother, Laura Testvalley proves constant. She can be trusted to understand what is important, to arrange what is needed, to be available when called.

When the book opens, Nan's is one of three families of American girls watering at Saratoga whose mothers are liabilities to their daughters' social advancement. Lizzie Elmsworth's mother lacks polish. The mother of the sensuously beautiful Conchita Closson is a divorced and remarried Brazilian woman who stays in her room and smokes cigars. Nan's mother, lacking all real knowledge of society and terrified of associating with the wrong people, is capable only of sniffish negative reactions. Her "only way of guiding her children was to be always crying out to them not to do this or that" (10). She is especially incompetent to perform the important maternal function of placing her daughters on the marriage market.

The families are nouveau riche and socially insecure. They have tried to set their daughters up for advantageous marriages by buying expensive houses in New York and taking them to fashionable spas, but their efforts are unproductive. Laura Testvalley proposes taking the girls to England to remove them from their mothers' social scene. Since she has European connections and has "finished" the daughters of an English duchess, she is able to convince all three families that their girls would benefit from a London social season. Together the young ladies will "invade" England to capture titled husbands. Miss Testvalley leads the invasion "like a general." Her strategies produce dazzling social opportunities for all of the girls despite the social liabilities of their families.

All four buccaneering girls make society marriages in England. Conchita weds a scapegrace young nobleman who had once been for a brief period the lover of Laura Testvalley. Very promptly the young couple become unfaithful to each other. Lizzie Elmsworth marries a titled business man and Member of Parliament. Virginia, Nan's beautiful sister, captures a dull nobleman with whom she is quite content. According to Wharton's plot summary, Nan, "the least beautiful but by far the most brilliant and seductive of them all . . . captures the greatest match in England, the young Duke of Tintagel" (358), ominously named for the husband whom Iseult wishes to leave because of her love for Tristan.

Nan's fairy tale unravels when her marriage turns out to be emotionally unsatisfying. The vibrant young Nan has subjected her free spirit to an ordered British life with the decent but dull Duke and his mother, the dowager duchess. The particulars of Nan's relationship to this mother-in-law receive considerable attention in the novel.

As an inexperienced American girl, she has fallen under the authority of Tintagel's mother, who faults Nan's social sense and her failure to provide heirs. The Tintagel dowager seems a judgmental presence to the entire household, all of whom "knew that her Grace's eye was on them," even though she has removed herself to the dower-house and is perfectly tactful. Much like Wharton's mother, the dowager duchess has "the awful gift of omnipresence, of exercising her influence from a distance" (275). Nevertheless, the author suggests that this disapproving mother-in-law contributes something valuable to Nan's maturation. Her subjugation to a regulated British life and the constraints of the dowager duchess provide the order and limits she needs if she is to control her unruly passions.

Having lost all joie de vivre and feeling cut off from the vital girl she had always been, Nan becomes alternately depressed and rebellious. Reluctantly, she comes "to see the use of having one's whims and one's rages submitted to some kind of control" (296). This "holding environment" proves to be a salutary stage in her development.

Much like Trollope's Glencora Palliser and a great deal like Edith Wharton, Nan has come to feel trapped in a dessicated marriage. Feeling inauthentic as Tintagel's Duchess, Nan compares herself inwardly to Goethe's Clärchen. She longs for the solace of her former governess, who had departed immediately after Nan's marriage to work with another family. Feeling depersonalized and isolated, Nan (now called more formally by her full name, Annabel) thinks:

> The real break with the vanished Annabel had come, the new Annabel sometimes thought, when Miss Testvalley, her task at the St. Georges' ended, had vanished into the seclusion of another family.... Perhaps Annabel thought, if her beloved Val had remained with her, they might between them have rescued the old Annabel, or at least kept up communications with her ghost—a faint tap now and then against the walls which had built themselves up about the new Duchess. But as it was, there was the new Duchess isolated in her new world, no longer able to reach back to her past, and not having learned how to communicate with her present. (262)

In order to maintain continuity with her old self and to carry it forward into full womanhood, Nan needs further contact with her psychological mother, the governess.

Like an ideal mother, Laura responds to Nan's call and returns in her time of need. On seeing Laura, the miserable young wife throws herself "on the brown cashmere bosom which had so often been her refuge. 'Of course you know, you darling old Val. I think there's nothing in the world you don't know.' And her tears broke out in a releasing shower" (335). Laura, who has in the meantime ripened physically and emotionally through an autumnal love affair of her own, will help release Nan from the prison of a loveless marriage and free her to find a joyous one with Guy Thwarte.

During her absence from Nan, Laura has captured the attentions of Guy Thwarte's father, an aging rake now ready to settle down. Under the love of this self-centered libertine, the forty-year-old governess blossoms physically: her eyes blaze, her skin glows, and her braided hair loosens into soft waves.

Wharton makes it very clear that middle-aged love can revital-
ize and empower a woman, even when the object of her love is
less than admirable. Passion spreads its healing unction outward to the very skin and hair, like a banner for all to see.
(Similarly, signs of sexual fulfillment become noticeable in
the much younger Conchita, who has always resembled a
glowing peach but becomes especially ripe after she takes on
an adulterous relationship.)

Laura helps Nan to break free of her marriage and run off
with Guy Thwarte, but at the cost of her opportunity to marry
Guy's father. Sir Helmsley Thwarte has political plans for his
son that are not compatible with the scandal of Guy's taking
up with the duke's wife, and he becomes enraged with Laura.
Knowing the consequences to herself, nevertheless, "the great
old adventuress, seeing love, deep and abiding love, triumph
for the first time in her career," promotes Nan's sexual fulfillment at the cost of her own (359).[5]

Through frank imagery the novel expresses the consequences of neglected sexuality. At the Temple of Love situated
on the mossy banks of the Love River, Guy surprises his deso-
late Nan:

> On the summit of the dome the neglected god [of love] spanned
> his bow unheeded, and underneath it a door swinging loose on
> broken hinges gave admittance to a room stored with the rem-
> nants of derelict croquet-sets and disabled shuttlecocks and
> graceless rings. It was evidently many a day since the lords of
> Longlands had visited the divinity who is supposed to rule the
> world. (317–18)

With Laura's help, Guy, newly returned from Brazil to his
family estate (called Honourslove), will rectify the neglect of
Eros. We might say that in this last novel Wharton enjoyed
honoring love in all its meanings.

In the course of the novel, the governess "finishes" Nan by
leading her first from virginal adolescence into marriage and
society and then out of her sterile marriage into the Temple
of Love, bringing her finally into blooming womanhood with

a true and understanding partner, although his surname, Thwarte, is troubling in this context. Nan is made to pass from her family into an empty marriage, must experience the desolation of having committed herself to a life of love-lessness, and then, out of her despair, find the strength to choose love at any price.

Thus Wharton rewrites the conclusion of Tristan and Iseult, allowing Nan to choose love over duty, to free herself perma-nently from the Duke of Tintagel. In so doing Wharton also rewrites the conclusion of her own poem, "Ogrin the Hermit," which, in portraying Iseult's return to lawful marriage, dra-matizes the conflict of love and duty, the sense of marriage as a prison. Except for the happy ending, the events of *The Bucca-neers* poignantly echo those of Edith Wharton's amative expe-rience. Unlike Wharton, Nan has at her side an ally who en-ables her to reject married imprisonment with Tintagel while still relatively young.

Laura's own rejuvenation through autumnal love puts her squarely on the side of passion. The author reinforces the theme of the older woman's right to passion by echoing it in the figure of Miss March, a sixty-year-old expatriate Ameri-can. The girls have to stretch their imaginations to envision a younger Miss March who might once have loved and been lovable. Only Laura and Nan do not ridicule the idea that this quaint older lady has once been in love. Conchita offers to amuse the girls with Miss March's love story:

> "I'll tell you something funny. . . . She was madly in love with Lord Brightlingsea—with my father-in-law. Isn't that a good one?" . . .
> "Mercy! In love? But she must be sixty," cried Virginia, scan-dalized.
> "Well," said Nan gravely, "I can imagine being in love at sixty." (124)

The girls are troubled by Miss March's apparent lack of self-respect in visiting the family of Lord Brightlingsea, who now scarcely remembers who she is. At each of Miss March's

visits, the self-centered gentleman who had once been engaged to her has to be reminded by his wife and daughters
that he has even met her before. "Nan sat brooding in her
corner. 'I think it just shows she loves him better than she
does her pride' " (124–25). The bitterness injected into this
light-hearted novel by recurring images of female passion con-
fronting male egotism and indifference seems to be a final
resurgence of the Fullerton motif. Nan's and Laura's comprehension of Miss March's way of loving put the author's blessing on passion, even when it is not requited.

By buying Nan's growth with her own personal sacrifice,
Laura perfects herself in Wharton's conception of the motherly role. In losing her opportunity to marry Guy's father,
Laura sacrifices a precious chance to gain social elevation,
financial security, and companionship in her declining years.
Through this renunciation Laura avoids becoming Nan's
mother-in-law, thereby retaining the elective character of
their mother-daughter relationship. Furthermore, by sacrific-
ing her own sexuality and going "back alone to old age and
poverty" (359), Laura Testvalley abandons the amatory field,
leaving the female sexual role to her surrogate daughter. In
Wharton's oedipal world, the daughter can enter fully and
lovingly into marriage only if the mother-figure has not pre-
empted that role.

The "little brown governess" whose strong personality
Wharton felt took over the novel[6] might be called a revenant
of the author's own Nanny Doyley, a figure returned from the
past to meet new needs, to reconcile Wharton to her past
choices, and to protect her against what was yet to come, the
helplessness of old age. Even in its unfinished state, *The Buccaneers* seems to bring Wharton's career full circle, both as an
allusion to the Italian setting of her first novel, *The Valley of
Decision*, and as a testament from age to youth, a yielding of
place. In her own strange way, Wharton seems finally to have
located in herself elements of both Nan, the "motherless girl,"
and Laura Testvalley, the childless woman. If only at the last,
the two incomplete selves found each other.[7]

THE KINDNESS OF STRANGERS: "ALL SOULS"

Following the testimony of Wharton's friends and the genial tone and calm resolution of *The Buccaneers*, biographers Lewis and Wolff detect a final mellowing or acceptance in Wharton's last years. They believe that she attained Eriksonian "integrity," or a benign sense of accepting the course of her own life.[8] But the terror of abandonment expressed in "All Souls," Wharton's very last story, suggests that even if she reached this state, she could not sustain it to the end.

One may reach moments of "integrity" or acceptance of one's own life, as Erik Erikson defined it, but be unable to maintain this attitude if one lacks a secure basis for trust, especially if one lives long enough to experience renewed threats of disintegration. The final stage of life need not be seen as a unitary state; it may have instabilities and dynamic reversals. The aged person may need sequential self-narratives or "summings up" in expectation of death, an event that may feel imminent but turn out to be deferred.

If Wharton attained to the stage of Integrity, this achievement may have been more provisional than the grand final chord Erikson describes, more tied to the exigencies of the particular life moment. She may have experienced moods of benign acceptance infiltrated by moments of personal terror. She concluded *A Backward Glance* with the view that experience is a welter of interpenetrating moods: "though the years are sad, the days have a way of being jubilant" (379).

"All Souls," completed about six months before her death, takes place on the last evening of October, All Souls Night, when, according to ancient beliefs, the dead can return to mingle with the living. Sara Clayburn is an elderly but independent widow who insists on occupying her large, isolated country house with the company of only a few family servants. Returning home from a walk on All Souls Eve, she has a disturbing encounter with an unknown woman who approaches the mansion seeking a visit with one of the servants. Mrs. Clayburn then slips on a frozen puddle, breaks her ankle, and is put to bed under strict medical orders not to use the injured foot. Her maid Agnes tries to leave a tray of food and drink on her night table, but Mrs. Clayburn declares that she does not eat during the night and does not want food near the bed. Agnes removes the tray but leaves it elsewhere in the room, creating a suspicion that she intends to be gone for a while and will not be there at her mistress's call at this time of special need.

Mrs. Clayburn awakens in what seems to be an empty house, cold, and unattended. Electricity seems to be cut off, the telephone does not work, and the disabled woman, hobbling about the house in search of the people she now needs more than ever, finds no one. Snow is falling; there is no fire in the grates nor heat in the pipes; the house is tidy, but cold, silent, and empty, like a sepulcher. She finds the servants' beds unused, but sees their clothing still hanging in the closets. They seem to have conspired to deceive her. She feels terrified and abandoned just when she most needs help.

She consumes the food left by Agnes, falls asleep, and finally awakens to the voice of her doctor and the faces of her servants. Agnes denies having left the house. Sara Clayburn's day and night of lonely terror are validated by no one; the one person who could have confirmed her story is unreachable. Like the Black Mass attended by Hawthorne's Young Goodman Brown, it may or may not have actually occurred, but whether it did or not, life will never again be the same.

A mysterious woman seems to have called away the servants and caused the mistress to be left cold and hungry, terrified by a foretaste of death. A year later the same woman reappears on All Souls Eve, and the servants are eager to go forth with her again. Mrs. Clayburn, whose very name suggests consumption of the flesh, flees her home forever to take up residence with her nearest relative, the cousin who narrates the tale. Rather than risk a third and probably final visitation with this strange woman, Sara Clayburn abandons her independent residence and takes shelter with someone of her own flesh and blood.

"All Souls" depicts the quintessential terror of almost every aging person, but especially of those who live alone—fear of a sudden transition from independence to helplessness. Living solitary, Mrs. Clayburn depends on the care of servants who are thoroughly devoted but must be assumed to have some lives and interests of their own. Their purchased services seem to the one dependent on them ultimately less reliable than the assistance of immediate family.

In this story the good servants resemble a nanny, who is free to leave service at any time and even when on duty has days off to pursue some life of her own. She has other loyalties, family of her own and perhaps a lover. Unlike a mother, she is not bound by blood always to be there when needed. The witching night of "All Souls," with its suggestions of debauchery and abandon, is, in Mrs. Clayburn's mind, the unknown but vaguely imagined private life of the servant women, something so powerful that it takes precedence over their responsibilities to her. She searches their bedrooms, finding unused beds but closets full of their clothes, evidence that they will return after having met their private needs. Like the clothes left behind by a nanny on her day off, these garments are both a reassurance and a threat. They promise the beloved caretaker's return, but testify to her essential independence of the needy one. To the nanny-reared child, this independence amounts to fear of abandonment. The child, like the disabled elderly woman, has no inalienable caretaker in whom to place its trust. Helplessness and fear of abandonment make old age much like infancy, but with the added disadvantages for the aged of having outlived the most dedicated and capable caretakers and of being less appealing to the nurturing instincts of others.

By 1937, when she wrote "All Souls," Edith Wharton's magnificent competence in worldly affairs seemed to have crumbled along with her health. She still mourned the loss of Walter Berry, now dead for ten years. Within a six-month period in 1933 death had claimed her trusted and beloved servants, Elise Duvlenck and Catherine Gross. A third servant was so upset by the losses that she departed. Wharton wrote to Mary Berenson just before Elise's death, "My poor Elise is failing slowly. . . . My old Gross is now quite mindless, but gentle & quiet, so I can settle her at the convent with the sisters; & as soon as Elise's sufferings are over I want to get away as quickly as I can from this House of Usher. . . . The strain on my heart-strings . . . is severe, for since Walter's death I've been incurably lonely *inside*, & these two faithful women kept the hearth-fire going" (May 26, 1933).

As in "All Souls," the absence of the servants presages death, the death of the house as well as a threat to the life of its owner. For Wharton hearth and heart were closely related words. Her hearth had long been tended by the kindness of strangers, faithful strangers who nevertheless eventually departed on business of their own. Their absence left the house static and cold, her inner self "incurably lonely" despite the attentions of many devoted friends. She could be distracted from her inner emptiness but could not fill it.

The return of the dead was often in Edith Wharton's mind during her last years. She dedicated *A Backward Glance* to "the friends who every year on All Soul's Night come and sit with me by the fire." At that time (1933), the visiting dead were friends whom she joyfully entertained at her hearth, the dear departed whom she welcomed back into the realm of the living. But four years later, when she wrote "All Souls," this mood of mellow acceptance was penetrated by fear. In this, her very last work, the revenant from the other world has become a figure of obscure threat, a female who lures the faithful to abandon those who trust them and beckons the abandoned one to follow her into the next world. Edith Wharton's final view was, I think, a mixture of both—on one level, serenity forged from her positive joy in existence and satisfaction with her own attainments, and on another, more primitive level, terror of entering alone and uncomforted into the unknown.

Appendix: "Beatrice Palmato"

Edith Wharton left among her papers these notes for a story that she never completed. Cynthia Griffin Wolff, who discovered them at the Bernicke Library at Yale University, calculates that they were written in 1919–20, whereas R. W. B. Lewis dates them around 1935.

PLOT SUMMARY

Beatrice Palmato is the daughter of a rich half-Levantine, half-Portuguese banker living in London, and of his English wife. Palmato, who is very handsome, cultivated and accomplished, has inherited his father's banking and brokering business, but, while leaving his fortune in the business, leads the life of a rich and cultivated man of leisure. He has an agreeable artistic-literary house in London, and a place near Brighton. The wife is handsome, shy, silent, but agreeable. There are two daughters and a son, the youngest. The eldest, Isa, who looks like her mother, commits suicide in mysterious circumstances at seventeen, a few months after returning from the French convent in which she has been educated. The mother has a bad nervous break-down, and is ordered away by the doctors, who forbid her to take little Beatrice (aged 12) with her. After a vain struggle, she leaves the child in the country with an old governess who has brought her up, and whom she can completely trust. The governess is ill, and is obliged to leave, and Beatrice remains in the country with her father. He looks for another governess, but cannot find one to suit him, and during a whole winter takes charge of Beatrice's education. She is a musical and artistic child, full of intellectual curiosity, and at the same time very tender and emotional; a combination of both parents. The boy, whom Mrs. Palmato adores, and whom her husband has never cared for, is a sturdy sensitive English lad. He is at school, and spends his holidays with his tutor. Mrs. Palmato is still abroad, in a sanitorium. The following autumn (after a year's absence) she comes home. At first she seems better, and they return to London, and see a few friends. Beatrice remains with them, as neither parent can bear to be separated from her. They find a charming young governess, and all seems well.

Then suddenly Mrs. Palmato has another nervous breakdown, and grows quite mad. She tries to kill her husband, has to be shut up, and dies in an insane asylum a few months later. The boy is left at school, and Mr. Palmato, utterly shattered, leaves on a long journey with Beatrice and a new maid, whom he engages for her in Paris. After six months he returns, and re-engages the same governess. Eighteen months after his wife's death he marries the governess, who is a young girl of good family, good-looking and agreeable, and to whom Beatrice is devoted.

The intimacy between father and daughter continues to be very close, but at 18 Beatrice meets a young man of good family, a good-looking rather simple-minded country squire with a large property and no artistic or intellectual tastes, who falls deeply in love with her.

She marries him, to every one's surprise, and they live entirely in the country. For some time she does not see her father or the latter's wife; then she and her husband go up to town to stay for a fortnight with the Palmatos, and after that they see each other, though at rather long intervals. Beatrice seems to her friends changed, depressed, overclouded. Her animation and brilliancy have vanished, and she gives up all her artistic interests, and appears to absorb herself in her husband's country tastes. The Palmato group of friends all deplore her having married such a dull man, but admit that he is very kind to her and that she seems happy. Once her father takes her with him on a short trip to Paris, where he goes to buy a picture or some tapestries for his collection, and she comes back brilliant, febrile and restless; but soon settles down again. After 2½ years of marriage she has a boy, and the year after a little girl; and with the birth of her children her attachment to her husband increases, and she seems to her friends perfectly happy. About the time of the birth of the second child, Palmato dies suddenly.

The boy is like his father, the little girl exquisite, gay, original, brilliant, like her mother. The father loves both children, but adores the little girl; and as the latter grows to be five or six years old Beatrice begins to manifest a morbid jealousy of her husband's affection for this child. The household has been so harmonious hitherto that the husband himself cannot understand this state of mind; but he humours his wife, tries to conceal his fondness for his little daughter, and wonders whether his wife is growing "queer" like her mother.

One day the husband has been away for a week. He returns sooner than was expected, comes in and finds the little girl alone in the drawing-room. She utters a cry of joy, and he clasps her in his arms and kisses her. She has put her little arms around his neck, and is hugging him tightly when Beatrice comes in. She stops on the threshold, screams out: "Don't kiss my child. Put her down! How dare you kiss her?" and snatches the little girl from his arms.

Husband and wife stand staring at each other. As the husband looks at her, many mysterious things in their married life—the sense of some hidden power controlling her, and perpetually coming between them, and of some strange initiation, some profound moral perversion of which he had always been afraid to face the thought—all these things become suddenly clear to him, lit up in a glare of horror.

He looks at her with his honest eyes, and says: "Why shouldn't I kiss my child?" and she gives him back a look in which terror, humiliation, remorseful tenderness, and the awful realization of what she has unwittingly betrayed, mingle in one supreme appeal and avowal.

She puts the little girl down, flies from the room, and hurries upstairs. When he follows her, he hears a pistol-shot and finds her lying dead on the floor of her bedroom.

People say: "Her mother was insane, her sister tried to kill herself; it was a very unfortunate marriage."

But the brother, Jack Palmato, who has become a wise, level-headed young man, a great friend of Beatrice's husband, comes down on hearing of his sister's death, and he and the husband have a long talk together—about Mr. Palmato.

The End

UNPUBLISHABLE FRAGMENT

"I have been, you see," he added gently, "so perfectly patient—"

The room was warm, and softly lit by one or two pink-shaded lamps. A little fire sparkled on the hearth, and a lustrous black bear-skin rug, on which a few purple velvet cushions had been flung, was spread out before it.

"And now, darling," Mr. Palmato said, drawing her to the deep divan, "let me show you what only you and I have the right to show each other." He caught her wrists as he spoke, and looking straight into her eyes, repeated in a penetrating whisper: "Only you and I." But his touch had never been tenderer. Already she felt every fibre vibrating under it, as of old, only now with the more passionate eagerness bred of privation, and of the dull misery of her marriage. She let herself sink backward among the pillows, and already Mr. Palmato was on his knees at her side, his face close to hers. Again her burning lips were parted by his tongue, and she felt it insinuate itself between her teeth, and plunge into the depths of her mouth in a long searching caress, while at the same moment his hands softly parted the thin folds of her wrapper.

One by one they gained her bosom, and she felt her two breasts pointing up to them, the nipples as hard as coral, but sensitive as lips to his approaching touch. And now his warm palms were holding each breast as in a cup, clasping it, modelling it, softly kneading it, as he whispered to her, "like the bread of the angels."

An instant more, and his tongue had left her fainting mouth, and was twisting like a soft pink snake about each breast in turn, passing from one to the other till his lips closed hard on the nipples, sucking them with a tender gluttony.

Then suddenly he drew back her wrapper entirely, whispered: "I want you all, so that my eyes can see all that my lips can't cover," and in a moment she was free, lying before him in her fresh young nakedness, and feeling that indeed his eyes were covering it with fiery kisses. But Mr. Palmato was never idle, and while this sensation flashed through her one of his arms had slipped under her back and wound itself around her so that his hand again enclosed her left breast. At the same moment the other hand softly separated her legs, and began to slip up the old path it had so often travelled in darkness. But now it was light, she was uncovered, and looking downward, beyond his dark silver-sprinkled head, she could see her own parted knees and outstretched ankles and feet. Suddenly she remembered Austin's rough advances, and shuddered.

The mounting hand paused, the dark head was instantly raised. "What is it, my own?"

"I was—remembering—last week—" she faltered, below her breath.

"Yes, darling. That experience is a cruel one—but it has to come once in all women's lives. Now we shall reap its fruit."

But she hardly heard him, for the old swooning sweetness was creeping over her. As his hand stole higher she felt the secret bud of her body swelling, yearning, quivering hotly to burst into bloom. Ah, here was his subtle fore-finger pressing it, forcing its tight petals softly apart, and laying on their sensitive edges a circular touch so soft and yet so fiery that already lightnings of heat shot from that palpitating centre all over her surrendered body, to the tips of her fingers, and the ends of her loosened hair.

The sensation was so exquisite that she could have asked to have it indefinitely prolonged; but suddenly his head bent lower, and with a deeper thrill she felt his lips pressed upon that quivering invisible bud, and then the delicate firm thrust of his tongue, so full and yet so infinitely subtle, pressing apart the close petals, and forcing itself in deeper and deeper through the passage that glowed and seemed to become illuminated at its approach . . .

"Ah—" she gasped, pressing her hands against her sharp nipples, and flinging her legs apart.

Instantly one of her hands was caught, and while Mr. Palmato, rising, bent over her, his lips on hers again, she felt his firm fingers pressing into her hand that strong fiery muscle that they used, in their old joke, to call his third hand.

"My little girl," he breathed, sinking down beside her, his muscular trunk bare, and the third hand quivering and thrusting upward between them, a drop of moisture pearling at its tip.

She instantly understood the reminder that his words conveyed, letting herself downward along the divan till her head was in a line with his middle she flung herself upon the swelling member, and began to caress it insinuatingly with her tongue. It was the first time she had ever seen it actually exposed to her eyes, and her heart swelled excitedly: to have her touch confirmed by sight enriched the sensation that was communicating itself through her ardent twisting tongue. With panting breath she wound her caress deeper and deeper into the thick firm folds, till at length the member, thrusting her lips open, held her gasping, as if at its mercy; then, in a trice, it was withdrawn, her knees were pressed apart, and she saw it before her, above her, like a crimson flash, and at last, sinking backward into new abysses of bliss, felt it descend on her, press open the secret gates, and plunge into the deepest depths of her thirsting body . . .

"Was it . . . like this . . . last week?" he whispered.

Notes

I quote Wharton's writings in text followed by parenthetical citations to page numbers, for the published materials, or dates, for the
letters. Page numbers refer to editions identified in the bibliography.
Where possible I quote Wharton's letters from *The Letters of Edith
Wharton*, ed. R. W. B. Lewis and Nancy Lewis, using dates attributed
by the editors. Letters I quote that were not included in this collection are identified parenthetically in text as from the Wharton manuscript materials in either the Ransom Center (Harry Ransom Humanities Research Center at the University of Texas at Austin) or the
Beinecke Library (Beinecke Rare Book and Manuscript Library, Yale
University).

"The Love Diary" is quoted from the manuscript in the Lilly Library, Indiana University. Letters from Morton Fullerton's mother
and his sister Katharine Fullerton Gerould are from the Fullerton
family papers (currently uncatalogued) in the Beinecke Rare Book
and Manuscript Library. Letters from Henry James to Edith Wharton are from *Henry James and Edith Wharton: Letters, 1900–1915*, ed.
Lyall H. Powers. James's letters to other recipients are from *Henry
James: Collected Letters*, ed. Leon Edel.

PREFACE

1. Jonathan Lear, *Love and Its Place in Nature: A Philosophical
Interpretation of Freudian Psychoanalysis*, 147.

2. Gloria C. Erlich, *Family Themes and Hawthorne's Fiction: The
Tenacious Web* (New Brunswick, N.J.: Rutgers University Press, 1984;
revised edition, 1986).

3. Sandra M. Gilbert and Susan Gubar, *The Madwoman in the
Attic: The Woman Writer and the Nineteenth-Century Literary Imagination*. See also Amy Kaplan, "Edith Wharton's Profession of Authorship," 433–57.

4. Although some of my conclusions are frankly speculative, they
accord, I believe, with the criteria of the hermeneutic psychoanalytic
method of case study, as defined by George E. Atwood and Robert
Stolorow in *Structures of Subjectivity: Explorations in Psychoanalytic
Phenomenology*. Structural analysis, in their view, is less concerned

with cause and effect than with "understanding of the interrelations linking different phenomena into strctural unities or wholes. . . . The adequacy of a structural explanation is measured not by its predictive power, but rather by the degree to which it brings together in one unitary interpretation domains that, at first sight, seem disconnected to the observer" (32–33).

5. This is stated emphatically in Sandra M. Gilbert and Susan Gubar, *Sexchanges*, 138 (vol. 2 of *No Man's Land: The Place of the Woman Writer in the Twentieth Century*).

INTRODUCTION

1. Jonathan Gathorne-Hardy, *The Rise and Fall of the British Nanny*, 30.

2. For an example of Gilman's thinking, see *The Home: Its Work and Influence* (New York: McClure, Philips, 1903).

3. Nancy Chodorow, *The Reproduction of Mothering: Psychoanalysis and the Sociology of Gender*, 28–29. See also Dorothy Dinnerstein, *The Mermaid and the Minotaur: Sexual Arrangements and Human Malaise*. An influential French historical treatment of motherhood that agrees with these two American works is Elisabeth Badinter, *Mother Love: Myth and Reality*. Badinter sums up her historical survey of motherhood as follows:

> A review of the history of different forms of maternal behavior gives birth to the conviction that maternal instinct is a myth. No universal and absolute conduct on the part of the mother has emerged. On the contrary, her feelings, depending on her cultural context, her ambitions, and her frustrations have shown themselves to be extremely variable. . . . Everything depends on the mother, on her history and our History. (327)

4. Joseph D. Lichtenberg, *Psychoanalysis and Infant Research*, 19.

5. In *The Interpersonal World of the Infant* Daniel N. Stern summarizes and elaborates on the research showing that infants have the capacity to recognize and remember many kinds of sensory configurations. See especially, pp. 92–93.

6. D. W. Winnicott, *The Maturational Processes and the Facilitating Environment: Studies in the Theory of Emotional Development*.

7. Harry T. Hardin, "On the Vicissitudes of Early Primary Surrogate Mothering," 627.

8. Louise Kaplan, *Oneness and Separateness: From Infant to Individual*, 383. The Kagan material is from "The Child and the Family," in *The Family*, the Spring 1977 issue of *Daedalus*, p. 36.

9. Hardin, "On the Vicissitudes of Early Primary Surrogate Mothering," 627. For Hardin's application of his theories to Freud, see his "On the Vicissitudes of Freud's Early Mothering," a three-part series in *Psychoanalytic Quarterly:* "I: Early Environment Loss" 56 (1987): 628–44; "II: Alienation from His Biological Mother" 57 (1988): 72–88; "III: Freiberg, Screen Memories, and Loss" 57 (1988): 209–23.

10. Hardin, "On the Vicissitudes of Early Primary Surrogate Mothering," 628.

11. Ibid., 626.

12. Lillian Smith, *Killers of the Dream,* 131–33.

13. Erik H. Erikson, *Identity: Youth and Crisis,* 103.

14. John Gedo, *Portraits of the Artist,* 96.

15. Judith L. Sensibar, *The Origins of Faulkner's Art,* 52. Relying on statements by John Faulkner, biographers Joseph Blotner (*Faulkner: A Biography,* 13) and Frederick Karl (*William Faulkner, American Writer: A Biography,* 57, 632) say that Caroline Barr (Mammy Callie) joined the Murry Falkner family when it moved to Oxford in 1902, about five years after William's birth. Relying on testimony from Jill Faulkner Summers and her half-brother Malcolm Franklin, Sensibar argues that Mammie Callie was in William Faulkner's life from the start (52–53, 237).

16. Karl, *William Faulkner, American Writer,* 632.

17. Ibid., 633.

18. Freud's early attachment to his nursemaid attracted some interest during the 1970s and is beginning to do so again. See Jim Swan, "*Mater* and Nanny: Freud's Two Mothers and the Discovery of the Oedipus Complex"; Kenneth Grigg, "All Roads Lead to Rome: The Role of the Nursemaid in Freud's Dreams," *Journal of the American Psychoanalytic Association* 21 (1973): 108–26; Marianne Krüll, *Freud and His Father* (New York: Norton, 1986); Paul C. Vitz, *Sigmund Freud's Christian Unconscious* (New York: Guilford Press, 1988).

19. Elisabeth Young-Bruehl, *Anna Freud: A Biography,* 35.

20. Ibid., 33, 34.

21. Ibid., 111.

CHAPTER I

1. My citations are to the manuscript version found in the Wharton collection, Beinecke Rare Book and Manuscript Library, Yale University, but "Life and I" has recently been published in *Edith Wharton: Novellas and Other Writings,* edited by Cynthia Griffin Wolff (New York: Library of America, 1990). The manuscript was written

around 1920–1922, according to Wolff in *A Feast of Words: The Triumph of Edith Wharton*, 417.

2. Peter Gay, *The Education of the Senses*, 278.

3. After the widowed Lucretia Jones moved to Paris, Edith seldom wrote and rarely visited her, even though she was often in the vicinity. By the time Lucretia died in 1901, Edith's twenty-ninth year, the two had been long estranged, and Wharton did not attend her mother's funeral. Indeed, Lucretia's last testament reflected her preference for her sons. She left most of her money directly to them; the balance was placed in a trust to be divided among the three, with Edith's share to be administered by brother Harry and another man. See R. W. B. Lewis, *Edith Wharton: A Biography*, 101.

4. Louis Auchincloss, *Edith Wharton: A Woman in Her Time*, 18.

5. In *Women of the Left Bank: Paris, 1900–1940*, Shari Benstock describes *A Backward Glance*: "Thus one discovers the lapses, silences, and gaps in this autobiography to be revealing of a life that consistently wrote a fiction of itself, that sealed the ruptures in the psychic framework and overlooked the anachronistic nature of the lived life, giving priority to a consistent view of the life at the expense of troublesome introspection" (42).

6. Such a broad spectrum of terrors probably has more than one cause. Wharton believed that her terrors started in her ninth year, following hospitalization for a near-fatal episode of typhoid fever at a Black Forest spa. According to Lenore C. Terr, a psychiatrist specializing in childhood trauma, the isolation treatment used in such cases could have been so traumatic that Edith might have reenacted it emotionally throughout the rest of her life. Reconstructing medical practices of the time and place, Terr depicts a child in a strange place, cut off from parents and visitors to avoid contagion, so that her only relief from isolation was her white-robed doctor hovering in the doorway rather than entering. Terr argues that this experience is at the heart of Wharton's ghost stories—that the figure of the white-robed doctor in the doorway accounts for her fear of thresholds, and that the isolation of that sickroom caused her sense of imprisonment and isolation. Lenore C. Terr, "Childhood Trauma and the Creative Product," 551–57.

7. Quoted in Wolff, *Feast of Words*, 52.

8. Elaine Showalter, *The Female Malady: Women, Madness, and English Culture, 1830–1980*, 133.

9. The last observation is from the autobiography of Margaret Cleaves, written in 1886 and quoted in Showalter, ibid., 136.

10. Auchincloss, *Wharton*, 12–13.

11. Maud Howe Elliott, daughter of Julia Ward Howe, quoted in Auchincloss, ibid., 12.

12. The courtship of Wharton's parents is described fairly closely in *False Dawn*, one of the four novellas comprising *Old New York* (New York: Appleton, 1924).

13. A photograph of the salon of the Joneses' house in Newport shows two paintings of Edith on the wall.

14. In 1878 Mrs. Jones arranged and paid for the private publication in Newport of *Verses*, a volume of twenty-nine early poems by Edith Newbold Jones.

15. In view of Wharton's descriptions of Lucretia Jones's cutting words and scornful presence, one wonders how Susan Goodman reaches the conclusion that in *A Backward Glance* Wharton "makes her mother 'dumb' and 'blank,'" as well as "inarticulate." *Edith Wharton's Women: Friends and Rivals*, 22–23.

16. M. Jeanne Peterson, *Family, Love and Work in the Lives of Victorian Gentlewomen*. Indeed, this study of the lives of a group of "ordinary" upper-middle-class British women, as distinguished from extraordinary or gifted women, undermines the stereotypical image of the Victorian lady as a passive and powerless denizen of the "private sphere" who was inviolably innocent and was victimized by neurasthenic illnesses because of prolonged sexual repression. Peterson's picture is of healthy, even athletic, women who led active lives in the public sphere as well as in the home.

17. See *Leonardo da Vinci and a Memory of His Childhood* and *The Sexual Enlightenment of Children*, edited by Philip Rieff (New York: Collier, 1971).

18. "Life and I," 34–35.

19. The invitation is reproduced on page 49 of Auchincloss, *Wharton*.

20. Adrienne Rich, *Of Woman Born: Motherhood as Experience and Institution*, 245.

21. "A Little Girl's New York," 361.

22. Ibid.

23. *Artemis to Actaeon and Other Verses*, 28, 14.

24. Candace Waid, *Edith Wharton's Letters from the Underground: Fictions of Women and Writing*, 58–59.

25. "Life" appeared in *Atlantic Monthly* 102 (1908): 501–04 and was reprinted in *Artemis to Actaeon*, 7–13.

26. The "Beatrice Palmato" material included in the Appendix to this book has previously been published in Lewis's *Biography*, 544–48, and in Wolff's *Feast of Words*, 301–05. The manuscript material that Wharton called "Beatrice Palmato" is in two parts: a plot summary and a narrative scene she titled "Unpublishable Fragment."

27. See Appendix, p. 173.

28. Ibid., 176. According to Cynthia Griffin Wolff, who discovered the hitherto unnoticed Palmato fragments in the Beinecke Library, "We can venture with some certainty that the little girl attached more than casual phallic significance to the warm, bare hand that held hers. What is more, the sensation must have stimulated her excessively (for she went to such phobic lengths to repress it) and persisted in her imagination . . . and the very name "Palmato" suggests the jest of the 'third hand.' When the core fantasy emerges it bears these unmistakable signs of its origin." (*Feast of Words*, 307).

29. See Appendix, p. 174.

30. Although Cynthia Griffin Wolff insists on the fictionality of the Palmato materials (*Feast of Words*, 305), she also supplies the basis for an autobiographical interpretation: "The longing from which the girl had run . . . is a flaming, consuming love for the father, a fear of penetration that is inextricable from a desperate yearning for it" (307). I share Wolff's reluctance to speculate about such a private event for which there can be no record other than circumstantial, but I believe that a good deal of psychobiography is inevitably speculative. I regard the suicide of Beatrice Palmato less as "violent authorial retaliation" (308) against women for acts committed by men than as evidence of the now-recognized self-hatred of the incest victim.

31. See note 10 to Chapter 2 below.

32. See, for example, Leslie Fiedler, *Love and Death in the American Novel* (New York: Delta, 1960).

33. See Louise De Salvo, *Virginia Woolf: The Impact of Childhood Sexual Abuse on Her Life and Work*.

34. *Collected Short Stories of Edith Wharton*, vol. 1, ed. R. W. B. Lewis. While this book was in press, I learned through an essay in the Spring 1991 issue of *Edith Wharton Review*, "Neglected Areas: Wharton's Short Stories and Incest," that Barbara A. White also treats "The Dead Hand" as evidence that Wharton was an incest victim. Her essay is part of a forthcoming book, *Edith Wharton: A Study of the Short Fiction* (Twayne).

35. Waid, *Letters from the Underworld*, 199–200.

36. "Pomegranate Seed," *Scribner's Magazine* 51:3 (March 1912): 284–91.

37. Wharton used this adaptation from Apuleius in a letter to her publisher, Brownell (cited in Wolff, 205) *Feast of Words*, and in "Literature," a manuscript version of the Vance Weston novels in the Beinecke collection.

38. *Harper's Magazine*, March 1938, 357.

39. Percy Lubbock, *Portrait of Edith Wharton*, 54, 11.

40. In *Wharton's Women*, 4, Susan Goodman also recognizes the split between Wharton's sexual and professional gender identities.

CHAPTER 2

1. Expatriated in many senses of the word, she felt strongly identified with homelessness and in 1916 compiled a volume called *Book of the Homeless* to raise funds for people displaced by the war.

2. Letter to Royall Tyler, quoted in Lewis, *Biography*, 421.

3. I borrow the language "internal arena" from Joan Lidoff, "Another Sleeping Beauty: Narcissism in *The House of Mirth*," 538.

4. Although some attention has been paid to parallels between *The House of Mirth* and *Daniel Deronda*, the significance of this apparent influence deserves fuller attention. For a survey of the parallels, see Constance Rook, "Beauty in Distress: *Daniel Deronda* and *The House of Mirth*," 28–39.

5. The mercantile language of *The House of Mirth* has been discussed by Wai-Chee Dimock, "Debasing Exchange: Edith Wharton's *The House of Mirth*," 783–92. This dazzling essay charts the extensiveness of market values in this book and assumes that Wharton repudiates this mentality. But Dimock does not take into account the prevalence of this theme in Wharton's work and in her private vocabulary.

6. For the importance of a woman's turning thirty in *The House of Mirth*, see Elaine Showalter, "The Death of the Lady (Novelist): Wharton's *House of Mirth*."

7. Wolff, *Feast of Words*, 230–50.

8. Wolff gives full justice to the imperious self in *The Custom of the Country*, regarding it as evidence of Wharton's recognition of her right to demand satisfaction in life, but Wolff underestimates the asexuality of Undine's desires.

9. Lidoff, "Another Sleeping Beauty: Narcissism in *The House of Mirth*," 531.

10. Virginia Woolf's attitude toward herself as a result of incestuous abuse is particularly instructive in this regard. See De Salvo, *Virginia Woolf*. See also Judith Herman and Lisa Hirschman, *Father-Daughter Incest* (Cambridge: Harvard University Press, 1981), and Chapter 1, above.

11. In *Wharton's Women*, 57, Susan Goodman also observes the rhyming of the two scenes in which Lily is nurtured by other women. In these episodes, as in her book as a whole, Goodman treats female bonding and cooperation as the moral center of the action. I do not think that Wharton's fiction is driven by such moral didacticism or

that salvation results from Lily's refusal to blackmail Bertha Dorset through her love letters.

12. Gilbert and Gubar, *Sexchanges*, 130, 138, 132. The authors find that even Charity Royall's situation in *Summer* is "not idiosyncratic but representative in the Wharton canon, for from the start this writer's critique of her culture appears to have been designed to reveal the hopeless incompatibility between 'the established order of things' and the 'individual [female] adventure' " (136).

13. Lidoff, "Another Sleeping Beauty," 520.

14. Ibid., 538: "In *The House of Mirth* Wharton transforms a personal psychic despair into a pessimistic social determinism, *locating in society the forces of inevitable destruction of spirit that proceed from within.* . . . The internal arena of the author's sensibility becomes the demonstration ground of the social harms she criticizes; and the flawed structure of her novel, as much as her heroine's death, shows the debilitating effects of the constrictions on realistic self-assertion" (italics added).

15. Berger is quoted in Judith Fryer, *Felicitous Space: The Imaginative Structures of Edith Wharton and Willa Cather*, 98.

16. Like Margaret Mitchell's Rhett Butler, who recognized Scarlett O'Hara's self-centered motives but still wanted to provide for her, Rosedale could see through Lily's deceptions and still desire her.

17. In "Succumbing to the 'Literary Style': Arrested Desire in *The House of Mirth*," Clare Colquitt deals with Lily's relationship to these letters, suggesting that her two-year possession of Bertha's love letters indicates that Lily envies Bertha's sexual capacity.

18. Wharton's provisional title for this novel of failed intimacy was "The Year of the Rose."

CHAPTER 3

1. I borrow script terminology from psychologist Silvan S. Tomkins's essay, "Script Theory," in *The Emergence of Personality*, ed. J. Aronoff, A. I. Rabin, and R. A. Zucker (New York: Springer, 1987), 147–216, but I use the expression in a less technical sense.

2. From a review of the Lewis biography by Kenneth Clark, *Times Literary Supplement*, December 19, 1975.

3. R. W. B. Lewis thinks she was modeled on Vernon Lee (Viola Paget), a lesbian, an intellectual, and a friend of Wharton. *Biography*, 96. Amy Kaplan suggests the addition of George Eliot as a model; see "Edith Wharton's Profession of Authorship," 456.

4. Among the reports submitted by Wharton's friends to Percy Lubbock for use in writing his *Portrait of Edith Wharton* are various

speculations about the degree of her interest in and attraction to Catholicism. Noting the influence of Wharton's Catholic servants, Nicky Mariano believed that Wharton was close to conversion. Gaillard Lapsley acknowledged her growing sympathy for the rituals and practices of the church but doubted that she was able to overcome her rationalistic tendencies.

5. Sophie Freud, *My Three Mothers and Other Passions*. The chapter called "The Passion Experience" offers useful research on the role of passion in feminine psychology. According to Sophie Freud, "the accompanying joy, pain, and turmoil have often led to new levels of maturity and depths of understanding of the human experience. It seems that while passion involves a loss of control, it curiously enough also often can lead to a greater feeling of control over life" (35).

6. Leon Edel, *Henry James: A Life*, 374.

7. "The Love Diary," also called "The Life Apart" or "L'âme close," in the manuscript collection, Lilly Library, Indiana University.

8. Regarding the identity of her lover, Wharton managed to mislead even our most distinguished literary sleuths, including for a time both Leon Edel and R. W. B. Lewis. Biographers were deceived despite the fact that many of Wharton's friends believed that Berry could not have been her lover and that Fullerton was, according to unpublished notes of interviews recorded in the 1950s by George Markow-Totevy and now deposited with the Wharton papers in the Beinecke Library.

9. Lewis, *Letters*, 11.

10. Louise J. Kaplan, *Female Perversions*, 228–29.

11. Ibid., 210.

12. Ibid., 223.

13. Lewis, *Biography*, 186.

14. See ibid., 541. Some of these statements about Camille Chabert and other lovers of Morton Fullerton are challenged by Marion Mainwaring in a book in progress, *The Quest for Morton Fullerton*. For Mainwaring's challenge to many statements in the R. W. B. Lewis biography, see "The Shock of Non-Recognition," 1394.

15. Sophie Freud, *My Three Mothers*, 62.

16. Edited by R. W. B. Lewis and Nancy Lewis.

17. Aubyn's removal to Europe so as better to see her American lover anticipates Edith Wharton's emigration to Paris in 1908. Distance enhanced her depictions of American material.

18. Love letters feature prominently in *The House of Mirth*, "The Letters," and "'Copy.' "

19. See Clare Colquitt, "Unpacking Her Treasures: Edith Whar-

ton's 'Mysterious Correspondence' with Morton Fullerton," 73–107, for an especially good analysis of this epistolary relationship.

20. "Terminus," *Atlantic Monthly*, 1909, 844–48.

21. *Artemis to Actaeon and Other Verses*, 7 ff.

22. "A Failure," *Atlantic Monthly*, April 1880, 464–65.

23. Catherine Bancroft calls attention to Wharton's "troubled sense of her power position in a sexual relationship," as evidenced in a letter to Fullerton in which she refers to a game in which she rejects the opportunity of winning because "I want to lose everything to you!" Says Bancroft: Wharton's "images grope for a language in which to make women's sexuality their own country. . . . Wharton found a way to repossess the heightened connection to life she saw as the chief gift of her sexual awakening" ("The Clever Trader: Metaphors of Sexual Awakening in Edith Wharton's Poetry, 1908–1909," in *Edith Wharton: Critical Essays*, ed. Alfred Bendixen and Annette Zilversmit [New York: Garland, 1991]).

24. From Sonnet VI of "The Mortal Lease," in *Artemis to Actaeon*, in which the speaker turns away from the sacramental cup offered by the Moment, appears to have been influenced by Emerson's "Days," in which a speaker rejects gifts proffered by a figure representing a unit of time.

25. Letters from Julia Fullerton to William Morton Fullerton, in the Fullerton family collection, Beinecke Library; dated 1893, n.d.

26. Ibid.; the last two letters excerpted here are undated.

27. Ibid.

28. Without disclosing her evidence, Marion Mainwaring maintains that Katharine had always known of her adoption. I base my conclusion that she did not learn of it until adulthood on her undated letter to Fullerton saying "I broke open the envelope to tell you that at last I have heard from my father about my adoption. [He says that] he cannot conscientiously and in justice to himself and his family, consent to what I propose [marriage to Morton?]. . . . Why didn't some of you foresee all this and arrange it otherwise?" Wolff also places Katharine's awareness of her adoption at around age twenty-five, *Feast of Words*, 199. See also Lewis, *Letters*, 139.

29. Even Katharine's stylish wedding conveyed mother Fullerton's mixed message. She whined that Katharine will be more comfortable "for the efforts I have made. Of course the money had to come right out of the little we have saved. I don't know if it occurs to her that it was any sacrifice on our part" (June 1910).

30. Katharine Fullerton to William Morton Fullerton, August 21, 1899, October 13, 1899, in the Fullerton family collection, Beinecke Library.

31. Ibid., January 7, 1908.

32. William Morton Fullerton to [the Ranee of Sarawak?], n.d., in the Fullerton family collection.

33. "Blanche Roosevelt" to William Morton Fullerton, n.d., in the Fullerton family collection.

34. *Collected Papers* 4: 211 ff.

35. Sophie Freud, *My Three Mothers*, 56.

36. Memo book, in the collection of the Harry Ransom Research Center, University of Texas at Austin.

37. See James W. Tuttleton, "Mocking Fate: Romantic Idealism in Edith Wharton's *The Reef*," for a particularly good analysis of the prurience of Anna's imagination.

38. Feminist critics such as Cynthia Griffin Wolff tend to favor Sophy Viner because she shows initiative and seizes life. James W. Tuttleton, a more traditional and moralistic critic, chooses Anna Leath, praising her renunciation of the available lover in favor of an ideal of purity; see "Mocking Fate," 459–74. Also moralistic, but making a strong case for Anna's unrelenting pursuit of knowledge, is James Gargano in "Edith Wharton's *The Reef*: The Genteel Woman's Quest for Knowledge," 40–48.

CHAPTER 4

1. Teddy Wharton to Sally Norton, February 26, 1907, in the Edith Wharton Collection, Beinecke Library.

2. "Les Derniers Mots," rough handwritten notes taken by Elisina Tyler shortly before Wharton's death, possibly part of a sheaf of papers called "Dernier Journal d'EW," in the Wharton Collection, Beinecke Library.

3. Personal report to Louis Auchincloss, in *Wharton*, 94.

4. "Les Derniers Mots."

5. Percy Lubbock, *Portrait of Edith Wharton*, 54. Although Lubbock may have incorporated his own injured feelings into his portrait of Wharton, his perceptions of the contradictions of her character are extremely valuable.

6. "Les Derniers Mots."

7. Typed "Notes" or reminiscences of Edith Wharton, written by Beatrix Farrand, in the Auchincloss section of the Edith Wharton Collection, Beinecke Library.

8. "Les Derniers Mots."

9. Lubbock, *Portrait*, 43.

10. According to interviews conducted in the 1950s by George Markow-Totevy and now deposited with the Wharton materials in the

Beinecke Library, Wharton's surviving friends thought it impossible for her to have had a sexual relationship with such a man as Berry and knew that the lover was Morton Fullerton.

11. Lewis, *Biography*, 288, 344.

12. Letters numbered 17, 41, and 44, in *47 Unpublished Letters from Marcel Proust to Walter Berry* (Paris: Black Sun Press, 1930). Although this limited edition purports to contain English translations of the letters by Harry and Caresse Crosby, the translating is generally believed to have been the work of Proust's brother Robert. I quote from the translations in this dual-language edition.

13. "Les Derniers Mots."

14. See Lubbock, *Portrait*, 8: "She was herself a novel of his, no doubt in his earlier manner."

15. Lyall Powers, ed., *Henry James and Edith Wharton: Letters, 1900–1915*, 111.

16. For another decade she had the intermittent companionship of Walter Berry and her attentive circle of benedicks. Her most reliable emotional supports for the final stretch were a few woman friends, her niece Beatrix Farrand, her pet dogs, and her female servants.

17. This view challenges the established critical tradition, as represented by both R. W. B. Lewis and Cynthia Griffin Wolff, which holds that Wharton's work moved from criticism of social repression toward the acceptance of tradition as the preserver of civilization.

18. Wharton's preoccupation with incest was recognized by Wolff in *Feast of Words* and forcefully treated by Adeline R. Tintner in "Mothers, Daughters, and Incest in the Late Novels of Edith Wharton."

19. Benstock, *Women of the Left Bank*, 40.

20. Letter, March 1908.

21. Lewis, "The Question of Edith Wharton's Paternity," Appendix A of *Biography*, 535–39. Lewis provides the results of his investigation of the rumor and concludes that Wharton was most likely not illegitimate and did not originate the rumor herself. He entertains but dismisses the pertinent psychological reasons that she might have started the rumor.

22. I borrow the term "prodigal mother" from Tintner, "Mothers, Daughters, and Incest."

23. Little record seems to remain of Wharton's relationship to her own mother-in-law. R. W. B. Lewis reports that Teddy was living with his parents until his marriage and that he regarded his mother as "the most attractive woman I know." *Biography*, 50.

24. The pre-oedipal aspect of the relationship between Kate and Anne is described in Marianne Hirsch, *The Mother/Daughter Plot:*

Narrative, Psychoanalysis, Feminism, 118–21. Although I find much to admire in this book, I cannot agree with its emphasis on maternal subjectivity in *The Mother's Recompense*. The mother-daughter relationship here is so peculiar, the mother herself so much an unsatisfied daughter, that the book does not readily serve as illustration of a mother's subjectivity. Nor is the lover shared by mother and daughter readily viewed as a male interloper; Chris Fenno derives his power from the desires of the two women.

CHAPTER 5

1. Elizabeth Ammons, *Edith Wharton's Quarrel with America*, 189.

2. Lewis, *Biography*, 491.

3. In his biography Lewis refers on page 503 to the "odd, disguised form of autobiography" in these two novels but sees it more as a reprise of her "previous literary treatment or transcription of memories" than as a fresh reliving of the past.

4. *The Buccaneers* was published in 1938 with Wharton's preliminary plot sketch and an Afterword by her friend and literary executor, Gaillard Lapsley.

5. From Wharton's plot summary following the breaking-off of the manuscript.

6. For a whimsical statement of Laura Testvalley's autonomy, see Wharton, *A Backward Glance*, 200–203.

7. My language here plays off of and modifies that of Wolff, who finds a "rightness—of ultimate resolution—a . . . sense of the world being set in order. The 'motherless' girl and the childless woman have finally found each other." *Feast of Words*, 405.

8. Integrity is the final stage of Erik Erikson's epigenetic theory of the life cycle, as in *Identity: Youth and Crisis*, 139, and elsewhere in his work.

Bibliography

MANUSCRIPTS

"Life and I," manuscript version of *A Backward Glance*. Beinecke Rare Book and Manuscript Library, Yale University.

"The Life Apart," or "L'âme close," also known as "The Love Diary." Manuscript department, Lilly Library, Indiana University.

Edith Wharton Collection. Harry Ransom Humanities Research Center, University of Texas at Austin.

Edith Wharton Collection. Beinecke Rare Book and Manuscript Library, Yale University.

Morton Fullerton family papers. Uncatalogued, in the Wharton collection, Beinecke Rare Book and Manuscript Library.

WORKS BY EDITH WHARTON

The House of Mirth. New York: Scribner's, 1905.
Artemis to Actaeon and Other Verses. New York: Scribner's, 1909.
The Reef. New York: Appleton, 1912.
Summer. New York: Appleton, 1917.
The Age of Innocence. New York: Scribner's, 1920. Rpt., 1970.
A Son at the Front. New York: Scribner's, 1923.
The Spark. New York: Appleton, 1924.
The Old Maid. New York: Appleton, 1924.
The Mother's Recompense. New York: Appleton, 1925.
Hudson River Bracketed. New York: Grosset & Dunlap, 1929.
The Gods Arrive. New York: Appleton, 1932.
A Backward Glance. New York: Scribner's, 1933. Rpt., 1964.
"A Little Girl's New York." *Harper's Magazine*, March 1938, 356–64.
The Collected Short Stories of Edith Wharton. Edited by R. W. B. Lewis. 2 vols. New York: Scribner's, 1968.

"The Touchstone." In *"Madame de Treymes" and Others: Four Novelettes.* New York: Scribner's, 1970.

The Letters of Edith Wharton. Edited by R. W. B. Lewis and Nancy Lewis. New York: Scribner's, 1988. Wharton's letters quoted from this edition are dated in accordance with it, though the dates of many letters remain conjectural.

SECONDARY SOURCES

Ammons, Elizabeth. *Edith Wharton's Quarrel with America.* Athens: University of Georgia Press, 1980.

———. "Fairy Tale Love and *The Reef.*" *American Literature* 47:4 (January 1976): 613–28.

Atwood, George E., and Robert Stolorow. *Structures of Subjectivity: Explorations in Psychoanalytic Phenomenology.* Hillsdale, N.J.: Analytic Press, 1984.

Auchincloss, Louis. *Edith Wharton: A Woman in Her Time.* New York: Viking, 1971.

Badinter, Elisabeth. *Mother Love: Myth and Reality.* New York: Macmillan, 1981. Translation of *L'amour en plus.* Paris: Flammarion, 1980.

Bancroft, Catherine. "The Clever Trader: Metaphors of Sexual Awakening in Edith Wharton's Poetry, 1908–1909." In *Edith Wharton: Critical Essays,* edited by Alfred Bendixen and Annette Zilversmit. New York: Garland, 1991.

Bell, Millicent. *Edith Wharton and Henry James: The Story of Their Friendship.* New York: Braziller, 1965.

Benstock, Shari. *Women of the Left Bank: Paris, 1900–1940.* Austin: University of Texas Press, 1986.

Blotner, Joseph. *Faulkner: A Biography.* New York: Random House, 1984.

Chodorow, Nancy. *The Reproduction of Mothering: Psychoanalysis and the Sociology of Gender.* Berkeley and Los Angeles: University of California Press, 1978.

Colquitt, Clare. "Succumbing to the 'Literary Style': Arrested Desire in *The House of Mirth.*" *Women's Studies* 20:2 (November 1991): 154–62.

———. "Unpacking Her Treasures: Edith Wharton's 'Mysterious Correspondence' with Morton Fullerton." *Library Chronicle* 31: 73–107. Austin: University of Texas at Austin, 1985.

Dalsimer, Katherine. *Female Adolescence: Psychoanalytic Reflections on Literature.* New Haven: Yale University Press, 1986.

De Salvo, Louise. *Virginia Woolf: The Impact of Childhood Sexual Abuse on Her Life and Work*. Boston: Beacon, 1989.

Dimock, Wai-Chee. "Debasing Exchange: Edith Wharton's *The House of Mirth*." *PMLA* 100 (1985): 783–92.

Dinnerstein, Dorothy. *The Mermaid and the Minotaur: Sexual Arrangements and Human Malaise*. New York: Harper & Row, 1976.

Edel, Leon. *Henry James: A Life*. New York: Harper's, 1985.

———, ed. *Henry James: Collected Letters*. Cambridge: Harvard University Press, 1987.

———. "Summers in an Age of Innocence: In France with Edith Wharton." *New York Times Book Review*, June 9, 1991.

———. "Walter Berry and the Novelists." *Nineteenth-Century Fiction* 38:4 (March 1984): 514–28.

Erlich, Gloria C. *Family Themes and Hawthorne's Fiction: The Tenacious Web*. New Brunswick: Rutgers University Press, 1984; revised edition, 1986.

Erikson, Erik H. *Identity: Youth and Crisis*. New York: Norton, 1968.

Fetterley, Judith. "'The Temptation to be a Beautiful Object': Double Standard and Double Bind in *The House of Mirth*." *Studies in American Fiction* 5 (1977): 199–211.

Freud, Sigmund. *Collected Papers*. Vol. 4. London: Hogarth Press, 1953.

———. *Leonardo da Vinci and Memory of His Childhood*. Translated by Alan Tyson. New York: Norton, 1964.

Freud, Sophie. *My Three Mothers and Other Passions*. New York: New York University Press, 1988.

Fryer, Judith. *Felicitous Spaces: The Imaginative Structures of Edith Wharton and Willa Cather*. Chapel Hill: University of North Carolina Press, 1986.

Gargano, James. "Edith Wharton's *The Reef*: The Genteel Woman's Quest for Knowledge." *Novel* 10 (Fall 1976), 409–48.

Gathorne-Hardy, Jonathan. *The Rise and Fall of the British Nanny*. London: Hodder and Stoughton, 1972.

Gay, Peter. *The Education of the Senses*. Vol. 1 of *The Bourgeois Experience: Victoria to Freud*. New York: Oxford University Press, 1984.

Gilbert, Sandra M., and Susan Gubar. *The Madwoman in the Attic: The Woman Writer and the Nineteenth-Century Literary Imagination*. New Haven: Yale University Press, 1979.

———. *Sexchanges*. Vol. 2 of *No Man's Land: The Place of the Woman Writer in the Twentieth Century*. New Haven: Yale University Press, 1989.

Goodman, Susan. *Edith Wharton's Women: Friends and Rivals*. Hanover, N.H.: University Press of New England, 1990.

Hardin, Harry. "On the Vicissitudes of Early Primary Surrogate Mothering," *JAPA* 33:3 (1985): 609–29.

Heilbrun, Carolyn G. *Writing a Woman's Life.* New York: Ballantine, 1988.

Hirsch, Marianne. *The Mother/Daughter Plot: Narrative, Psychoanalysis, Feminism.* Bloomington: Indiana University Press, 1989.

Kaplan, Amy. "Edith Wharton's Profession of Authorship." *ELH* 53:2 (Summer 1986): 433–57.

Kaplan, Louise J. *Female Perversions: The Temptation of Emma Bovary.* New York: Doubleday, 1991.

———. *Oneness and Separateness: From Infant to Individual.* New York: Simon & Schuster, 1978.

Karl, Frederick R. *William Faulkner, American Writer: A Biography.* New York: Weidenfeld, 1988.

Klein, Melanie. *The Writings of Melanie Klein,* ed. R. E. Money-Kyrle, in collaboration with B. Joseph, E. O'Shaughnessy, and H. Segal. 4 vols. New York: Free Press, 1984.

Lear, Jonathan. *Love and Its Place in Nature: A Philosophical Interpretation of Freudian Psychoanalysis.* New York: Farrar, Straus & Giroux, 1990.

Lewis, R. W. B. *Edith Wharton: A Biography.* New York: Harper and Row, 1975.

Library Chronicle of the University of Texas at Austin, n.s. 31 (1985). Special issue on the Edith Wharton–Morton Fullerton correspondence in the collection of the Harry Ransom Humanities Research Center.

Lichtenberg, Joseph D. *Psychoanalysis and Infant Research.* Hillsdale, N.J.: Analytic Press, 1983.

Lidoff, Joan. "Another Sleeping Beauty: Narcissism in *The House of Mirth.*" *American Quarterly* 32 (1980): 519–39.

Lubbock, Percy. *Portrait of Edith Wharton.* New York: Appleton, 1947.

Mainwaring, Marion. "The Shock of Non-Recognition." *Times Literary Supplement,* December 16–22, 1988.

Nevius, Blake. *Edith Wharton: A Study of Her Fiction.* Berkeley and Los Angeles: University of California Press, 1953.

Peterson, M. Jeanne. *Family, Love, and Work in the Lives of Victorian Gentlewomen.* Bloomington: Indiana University Press, 1989.

———. "The Victorian Governess: Status Incongruence in Family and Society." In *Suffer and Be Still: Women in the Victorian Age,* edited by Martha Vicinus. Bloomington: Indiana University Press, 1972.

Powers, Lyall, ed. *Henry James and Edith Wharton: Letters, 1900–1915.* New York: Scribner's, 1990.

Proust, Marcel. *47 Unpublished Letters from Marcel Proust to Walter Berry.* Paris: Black Sun Press, 1930.

Rich, Adrienne. *Of Woman Born: Motherhood as Experience and Institution.* New York: Norton, 1976.

Rook, Constance. "Beauty in Distress: *Daniel Deronda* and *The House of Mirth.*" *Women and Literature* 4:2 (1976): 28–39.

Sachs, J. J. "The Maid: Her Importance in Childhood Development." *Psychoanalytic Quarterly* 40: 469–84.

Schriber, Mary Suzanne. "Edith Wharton: The Female Imagination and the Territory Within." In *Gender and the Writer's Imagination: From Cooper to Wharton.* Lexington: University Press of Kentucky, 1987.

Sensibar, Judith L. *The Origins of Faulkner's Art.* Austin: University of Texas Press, 1984.

Showalter, Elaine. "The Death of the Lady (Novelist): Wharton's *House of Mirth.*" In *Edith Wharton,* edited by Harold Bloom. New York: Chelsea, 1986.

———. *The Female Malady: Women, Madness, and English Culture, 1830–1980.* New York: Pantheon, 1985.

Smith, Lillian. *Killers of the Dream.* 1949; revised edition, New York: Norton, 1961.

Stern, Daniel N. *The Interpersonal World of the Infant: A View from Psychoanalysis and Developmental Psychology.* New York: Basic Books, 1985.

Swan, Jim. "*Mater* and Nanny: Freud's Two Mothers and the Discovery of the Oedipus Complex." *American Imago* 31 (1974): 1–64.

Terr, Lenore C. "Childhood Trauma and the Creative Product: A Look at the Early Lives and Later Works of Poe, Wharton, Magritte, Hitchcock, and Bergman." *The Psychoanalytic Study of the Child* 42, New Haven: Yale University Press, 1987.

Tintner, Adeline R. "Mothers, Daughters, and Incest in the Late Novels of Edith Wharton." In *The Lost Tradition: Mothers and Daughters in Literature,* edited by Cathy N. Davidson and E. M. Broner. New York: Ungar, 1980.

Tuttleton, James W. "Mocking Fate: Romantic Idealism in Edith Wharton's *The Reef.*" *Studies in the Novel* 19:4 (Winter 1987): 459–74.

Wagner-Martin, Linda. "A Note on Wharton's use of *Faust.*" *Edith Wharton Newsletter* 3:1 (Spring 1986): 1.

Waid, Candace. *Edith Wharton's Letters from the Underground: Fictions of Women and Writing.* Chapel Hill: University of North Carolina Press, 1991.

White, Barbara A. "Neglected Areas: Wharton's Short Stories and Incest." *Edith Wharton Review* 8:1 (Spring 1991): 3–11.

Winnicott, D. W. *The Maturational Processes and the Facilitating Environment: Studies in the Theory of Emotional Development.* Madison, Conn.: International University Press, 1965.

Wolff, Cynthia Griffin. *A Feast of Words: The Triumph of Edith Wharton.* New York: Oxford University Press, 1977.

Young-Bruehl, Elisabeth. *Anna Freud: A Biography.* New York: Summit Books, 1988.

Acknowledgments

My research on Edith Wharton has been aided by the following grants, for which I am very appreciative: a fellowship as Visiting Scholar with the Blanche, Edith, and Irving Laurie New Jersey Chair in Women's Studies at Douglass College of Rutgers University; a travel-to-collections grant from the National Endowment for the Humanities to use the Edith Wharton archives in the Harry Ransom Humanities Research Center at the University of Texas at Austin; a fellowship as Visiting Scholar at the Beinecke Rare Book and Manuscript Library of Yale University; and a yearlong fellowship from the American Council of Learned Societies.

Passages from Edith Wharton's unpublished manuscripts are quoted with the kind permission of the above-named libraries and of the Lilly Library of Indiana University and the Edith Wharton estate. "Beatrice Palmato" is reprinted here with the permission of the Edith Wharton estate. The letter by Morton Fullerton is quoted with permission from Marion Mainwaring. Letters from Julia Fullerton and Katharine Fullerton Gerould are quoted with permission from Olivia Thorne.

An early version of Chapter 3 appeared as "The Sexual Education of Edith Wharton" in *Literature and Psychology* 36:1 and 2 (1990): 26–47, and is used here with the permission of the editors. "The Libertine as Liberator: Morton Fullerton and Edith Wharton," from *Reading the Letters of Edith Wharton*, a special issue of *Women's Studies* 20:2 (November 1991): 97–108, is used with permission of the editors (copyright © Gordon and Breach Science Publishers, S.A.). I am especially grateful for the generosity of Judith Hancock, the indexer of this book, a Wharton enthusiast, and formerly a colleague in the Princeton Research Forum, for valuable suggestions and for the loan of her collection of Edith Wharton first editions as well as copies of uncollected Wharton poems.

The Biography Seminar of New York University has been for almost ten years a source of colleagueship and encouragement. An early version of Chapter 3 was presented before this group. One member, Richard Goldstone, very generously lent me his copy of the rare limited edition of *47 Unpublished Letters from Marcel Proust to Walter Berry.*

The Edith Wharton Society has contributed a great deal to my understanding through its *Edith Wharton Review* and its superb conferences that bring Wharton scholars together. Among individual members of the society, Clare Colquitt, the late Joan Lidoff, and Annette Zilversmit have been especially helpful. Candace Waid generously gave me page proofs of her *Edith Wharton's Letters from the Underground: Fictions of Women and Writing* while it was in press.

For reliable intellectual support and encouragement in all my work, I warmly thank Rae Carlson, a professor of psychology at Rutgers University. For critical readings and valuable suggestions on various phases of this manuscript, appreciation goes to Ellen Friedman, Trenton State College, and James Tuttleton, New York University. Most particularly, I thank my husband, Philip Erlich, who has encouraged and facilitated my work in countless ways.

Seeing this book to completion with the staff of the University of California Press has been a pleasurable collaboration. From the start, I received from editor Doris Kretschmer and the staff the confident feeling that my book had found its proper home. For a brilliant job of copy editing by Ellen Stein I wish to express my highest admiration.

Index

Incest: and the "Beatrice
Palmato" fragment, 100, 126,
182n30; in "The Cenci" (Shelley), 146; and Fullerton, xii,
99, 100–101; in *The House of
Mirth*, 61–62, 74; in *Hudson
River Bracketed* and *The Gods
Arrive*, 154; in *The Mother's
Recompense*, 145–46; research
about, 183n10; in *Summer*,
126–31; and Virginia Woolf,
40, 183n10; Wharton's preoccupation with, 188n18; and
Wharton's sexual fantasies,
31, 33, 36–39, 40, 41–42, 45,
74, 88, 100–101, 125–26, 141;
Wharton as a victim of,
182n34. *See also* Oedipal
theme
Intimacy, 7, 30, 59, 92–93, 118,
184n18
Isador, Ladislas (fictional character), 39–40

James, Henry: and Berry, 119,
120; death of, 124; and Fullerton, 86, 87, 88, 89, 90–91, 124;
and homosexuality, 90–91; social class of, 20; Wharton's relationship with, 91, 118, 121–
24; writings of, 41, 108
Jews, 39–40, 73–74. *See also*
Rosedale, Simon
Jones, Frederic (brother), 22
Jones, George Frederic (father):
death of, 37, 55; as an indifferent father, 26–27; introduces
Wharton to poetry, 14, 32–33,
125–26; as a model for Wharton's writings, 21, 54–55,
142–44, 181n12; personal
background of, 16, 21, 31,
181n12; wasted talent of, 32–

33, 139–40; and Wharton's artistic creativity, 14, 141; Wharton's idealization/admiration,
14, 22, 23, 31, 54, 55, 125; and
Wharton's paternity, 31, 141,
188n21; Wharton's relationship with mother and, 18, 32–
35, 40, 45, 47–48, 125, 139;
and Wharton's sexual fantasies, 14, 31, 36–39, 40, 45, 74,
125, 141; Wharton's unre-
solved feelings about, 74; and
Wharton's views of femininity,
14, 31–32, 47–48, 54, 125
Jones, Henry (brother), 22, 46,
180n3
Jones, Lucretia Stevens Rhinelander (mother): as the bad
mother, xi–xii, 14, 18, 23–30,
141, 181n15; and *The Buccaneers*, 158–66; as a caring
mother, 25–26; and the censor-
ing of Wharton's reading, 33;
and clothes, 21; death of, 76,
180n3; familial economic circumstances of, 21, 32; as an
indifferent mother, 26–27;
marriage/courtship of, 21, 31,
181n12; as a model for *The
House of Mirth*, 54–55, 67; omnipresence of, 28, 125, 126;
and the publication of Wharton's poetry, 26, 181n14; role
in Wharton's delayed sexual
maturation, ix, xii, 16; social
prominence of, 16, 21, 67;
Wharton's adult relationship
with, 76, 180n3; Wharton's
feelings about, 21, 24, 30, 47,
76; and Wharton's gender
split, 47–48; Wharton's portrayal of, 21, 22, 23; and Wharton's relationship with her fa-

Compositor:	Huron Valley Graphics
Printer:	Haddon Craftsmen
Binder:	Haddon Craftsmen
Text:	10/13 Aster
Display:	Aster